PETER MINTO

THE FLYING
SPORTSMAN

A BIOGRAPHY OF FNS CREEK

*The life and legacy of a
forgotten sporting hero*

Published by Mereo

Mereo is an imprint of Memoirs Publishing

1A The Wool Market Cirencester Gloucestershire GL7 2PR
info@memoirsbooks.co.uk   www.memoirspublishing.com

THE FLYING SPORTSMAN
A Biography of FNS Creek

ISBN: 978-1-86151-030-3

Printed and bound in Great Britain by
Marston Book Services Ltd, Oxfordshire

CONTENTS

Acknowledgements
Foreword

ACKNOWLEDGEMENTS

A number of people and institutions helped me in the writing of this book. However, three individuals in particular deserve special mention:

Carey Creek, son of Norman, who was so patient in answering my many letters and telephone calls, and also sent me a copy of his father's WW1 flying log.

Jamie Roberts, grandson of Norman, with whom I have had much email correspondence and who photocopied for me his grandfather's scrapbooks.

Lucy Roberts, grand-daughter of Norman, who shared her memories of him with me.

Many others answered my requests for information or suggested lines of enquiry, and I am very grateful to them:

Barry Aitken, member of Wiltshire Query's; George Almond; Revd. Gordon Bates, vicar at Orsett Church Centre, Essex; Peter Butters; Peter Capon, Archivist, The Museum of Army Flying; Revd. Simon Crawley, former vicar at Folkestone; Darlington Library, Local Studies Section; Dauntsey's School, Wiltshire; Julie

Romijn, Foundation Office Secretary and Doreen Campbell, Archivist; Cecilia and Colin Dean; Geoffrey Dean; Frank Dobson; Nicola Edwards, *The Folkestone Herald*; Tim Fisher, Principal, Sixth Form College, Darlington; David Foot; Mike Greenwood; Revd. E.W. Hanson, Vicar at United Benefice of Orsett, Bulphan and Horndon-on-the-Hill, Essex; Revd. Mark Hayton, Vicar, The Trinity Benefice, Folkestone; Pamela Hayton; Derek Lewin; David and Neil Minto; Andy Palmer, Head of Cricket, Dauntsey's School; Mike Pinner; Terry Robinson; David Smith; Jonathan Smith, Archivist, Trinity College, Cambridge; *The Northern Echo*; Bob Thursby.

Last, but by no means least, my thanks to my wife Christine for her enthusiasm, encouragement and her honest and always constructive criticism. Without her the book most certainly would not have been written.

The following books proved useful: *World Aircraft, Origins – World War 1* by Enzo Angelucci and Paolo Matricardi; *Play Up Corinth*, by Rob Cavallini; *Boots, Balls and Haircuts*, by Hunter Davies; *A History of Cricket* by Benny Green; *The Wisden Book of Cricketers' Lives*, compiled by Benny Green; *Aces Falling – War above the Trenches, 1918*, by Peter Hart; *English Football – The Complete Illustrated History*, by Robert Jeffery; Somme, by Lyn Macdonald; *The Victorian Vision*, edited by John M. Mackenzie; *GB United?*, by Steve Menary; *The Paris Gun*, by Henry W. Miller; *In Peace and War –*

Memoirs of Herbert and Robin Rowell, edited by Elizabeth Rowell; *A Century of Elementary Education in Darlington*, by Stockdale; *On the Corinthian Spirit*, by D J Taylor; *In Flanders Fields*, by Leon Wolff.

FOREWORD

In January 1997 a parcel arrived at The Queen Elizabeth Sixth Form College in Darlington, County Durham from Vancouver, Canada. It contained eight England international football caps (one of them for a full international against France, the others were for amateur international games). They had been awarded, in the 1920s and 30s, to F N S (Norman) Creek.

Norman Creek had been a student at the grammar school in the town, now the Sixth Form College. The caps had been given to the college by Norman's son, Carey, to be put on permanent display. The then Principal of the college was naturally delighted to receive them.

For me these caps became the starting point of a quest to find out more about the man who had won them. I had been a lifelong fan of football, but I had no knowledge of Norman Creek's achievements in the game. Little did I know that my search would reveal a man who had shone in many fields and become a household name. The more I learned about him, the more I felt the man and his achievements should be more widely known. Hence this book.

IN THE BEGINNING

The Diamond Jubilee of Queen Victoria on the 22nd of June 1897 was celebrated throughout the land with parades, music in parks, old English sports, children's fêtes and firework displays. As the *Times* reported, 'Town centres were bedecked with banners and flags, and houses in even the poorest streets had commemorative tokens hung out of windows, tacked to a pole, or strung across from house to house.'

Queen Victoria was more renowned throughout the world than any other monarch before her. During the Victorian Age education, healthcare and social reform had improved the lives of millions in this country and inventions in engineering and transport had radically changed communications, not only in Britain but in her expanding colonies. Darlington in County Durham, where the world's first passenger-carrying railway had run, was very much part of the transport revolution, and as its local paper stated, 'The town was no exception in this universal recognition of the glorious reign of Her Majesty and the grand accomplishments of the Victorian epoch'.

Seven months after the Jubilee, a more local celebration took place at 21, Greenbank Road, Darlington, one of a row of small 19th century terraced houses. There on the 12th January 1898, Arthur and Edyth Creek's first child was born. He was christened Frederick Norman Smith Creek and called by family and friends Norman, although in years to come, when his various exploits were chronicled, he would usually be referred to as F N S Creek. He was Victorian by birth (just). He became a child of Edwardian times and his early manhood was fashioned in the First World War, followed by a teaching career. He won international football caps and had success in many fields, as an author, broadcaster, Minor Counties cricketer, Assistant Director of Coaching for the Football Association and Manager and Coach of the Great Britain football teams in the 1956 and 1960 Olympic Games in Melbourne and Rome.

Creek was a man who achieved so much in so many areas that one wonders where his talents and determination came from. What was his background? His forebears did not originate from Darlington. The earliest available records of the Creek family show that in the mid 1830s the 80th (Staffordshire Volunteers) Regiment of Foot, which mainly recruited from its local area, was stationed in Ireland. Henry Frederick Creek was one of the soldiers, and while there he met and married a young Irishwoman named Matilda McKeiver. These were Norman's great grandparents. The regiment moved back to England, and in 1837 Henry and Matilda's first child, Jane, was born in Chatham, Kent.

From 1836 to 1838 detachments of the 80th were assigned as guards on convict ships sailing to the penal settlement in the developing colony of New South Wales in Australia. Henry, now a sergeant, travelled in one of the last of these, and Matilda and Jane went with him. The vessels were wooden three-masted barques and the journey took at least twenty weeks. For Henry this was simply part of his lot as a serving soldier, but for Matilda, with a two-year-old child to care for, it must have been something of an ordeal.

On arrival in New South Wales they lived first of all in barracks in Sydney, where the regiment's headquarters were located, but they were later moved to Parramatta, twelve miles inland. At this time, although there was still a penal settlement at Sydney, the colony of New South Wales and the adjoining area of South Australia were actively seeking an increase in their civilian population to work on the livestock and cereal farms, and also in the newly-opened silver, lead and copper mines. To achieve this, The Colonisation Commission had started placing advertisements in English newspapers offering assisted migration schemes.

For many families living on or near the poverty line

in Britain, the prospect of starting a new life in a developing country must have seemed very attractive. By 1840 more than three thousand people had taken advantage of the scheme. Although great strides had been made in the building of wharves, roads and bridges, the development of markets and banks, and the establishment of a constabulary, this was a part of Victoria's growing empire which was heavily dependent on the army in many respects. The penal settlement had to be controlled and order had to be kept in the small but growing towns, as well as in outlying stations such as Norfolk Island, where a convict riot had to be put down and dealings with aboriginal groups resolved. Henry, as a non-commissioned officer, would have been involved in many of these.

Matilda too had her hands full, as Jane now had two sisters, Anna, born in 1840, and Sarah, born in 1843. However, at that time there was a disturbing lack of capital in the colony. Expenditure was way beyond what the settlement could raise (in 1843 the Adelaide City Council had gone bankrupt) and the colonial governments couldn't meet their half of the cost of maintaining the troops. There was a subsequent reduction in troop numbers, with most of those who left Australia being reassigned to duties in India.

A few, including the Creek family, returned to England. Almost certainly this was due to health problems, as Henry was suffering from rheumatism and he left the army within two years of their arrival in

Tilbury Port in 1844. Their first son, Henry, was born in Tilbury in 1845. Very shortly after that, with Henry, the father, now out of the army, the family moved to northern England, making their home in East Thickley, a small hamlet near Shildon in County Durham, where their second son, William, was born in 1847.

It is not clear whether it was chance which drew them to South Durham, or the realisation that this was where a new industry was developing and there would be job opportunities. Certainly the heavy engineering works, linked to the embryonic railways, needed a large labour force. But the family was struck a cruel blow almost before they had settled in the area. On the 18th of May, 1847, Henry Frederick, aged 39, died of 'spasms of the heart'. Matilda, now a widow of 37, was left with the task of supporting herself and the five young children aged between 10 years and a few months.

She had dressmaking skills, and took in lodgers, mainly young men who had come to the area to find work as railway labourers. By these means she was able to keep the family together, and ten years later the financial pressures eased, as the two eldest daughters, Jane and Anna, had moved out, Henry was working as a clerk at the Shildon Engine Works and William was an apprentice engine fitter, while Sarah helped at home.

The Creek family was now on an even keel at the lower working-class level of society. The steady climb to middle-class status started with the efforts of Henry, the railway clerk. Henry had moved to Darlington, where he married Mary, a Darlington girl. Their eldest child, Arthur Frederick, was born in 1871, and after attending Bondgate Wesleyan School in the town and then the Boys' Grammar School, he followed his father onto the clerical staff of the North East Railway Company. In 1896 Arthur married Edyth Smith and they set up home in Greenbank Road (later renamed Greenbank Crescent) in Darlington, where their three sons were born, including Frederick Norman Smith, the eldest and the subject of this biography.

By the end of his career with the NER, Arthur had risen to be a member of the North East Locomotive Accountants and also taken on the role of secretary of the Darlington General Hospital. This upward mobility in the family's fortunes, due in large part to Arthur's hard work and determination, was further enhanced through his active involvement in Freemasonry (he was a founder member and then Master of both the St Cuthbert and Trinity Lodges in the town). The 1911 census showed that Arthur, Edyth and their family also had a female servant living with them. The status of the family had risen again, and when Arthur retired in 1932 they moved to a more desirable house in Carmel Road South.

Arthur's grandmother, Matilda, would have been very proud of what her grandson had achieved. It was almost inevitable then that education would be seen as of great importance and it is no surprise that Norman began his schooling at the Bondgate Wesleyan School near Greenbank Road. At that time, 1903, places there were much sought after by parents who had their eyes on their children being awarded one of the limited number of free places at The Queen Elizabeth Grammar School for Boys in the town. A fee of 3d per week was charged, even though fees in most elementary schools had ended.

In his last year at the Wesleyan school, Norman was entered for The George Stephenson Memorial Scholarship. This was set up to perpetuate the memory of the late George Stephenson who, when he died in 1881, had been Passenger and Goods Manager of the Darlington section of the North East Railway. It was open to boys under the age of 11 whose fathers were in the employ of the NER Company. Norman was successful, and in September 1909 he transferred to the Grammar School.

National regulations which had been introduced in 1904 for the four-year curriculum of secondary schools dictated that he followed four groups of subjects: English Language and Literature with History and Geography; at least one foreign language; Maths and Science (theoretical and practical); and Drawing. In addition, thanks to the sporting interests of the headmaster, football, athletics and cricket were also given some prominence.

Mr Philip Wood had been appointed head of the school in 1878 and retired in 1913, so Norman knew him only for the first four years of his grammar school career, but he could not have failed to be influenced by him. Wood was something of an eccentric. Dressed in his favourite greenish tweed Norfolk jacket and knickerbockers, he was often to be seen riding into town on his tricycle. On Wednesday afternoons in the cricket season he would umpire for the last hour of games sitting on his shooting stick surrounded by a ring of cigar stubs, as he was a chain smoker. Woe betide any bowler who asked him for a decision if it was blatantly not out, as he would give him an 'annihilating look'.

Fair play was expected of all who took part and that was certainly something that Norman took to heart. Philip Wood was also a scholar who had a First Class Honours degree in Mathematics from Edinburgh University and by encouraging the pursuit of academic excellence among the boys he gradually raised the standing of the school.

So in his formative years Norman, who was from a loyal, hard-working Christian household, was fortunate in having those family values supplemented by the values Mr Wood inculcated in his pupils. Norman was obviously a bright lad, as he entered the sixth form in 1914, having passed the recently inaugurated (in 1911) School Certificate. For the next two years he studied Maths, Chemistry and Physics. As well as an aptitude for academic study he was also showing above-average ability on the sports field, and in his final year he captained both the cricket and football teams. Matches were played against other grammar schools in the area, such as Bishop Auckland and Durham, and the private boarding school at Barnard Castle, in which he was able to display his prowess with both bat and ball.

On both the academic and sporting fronts the future looked rosy. However, more momentous things were happening on the world stage at that time. The outbreak of the First World War and the great numbers of young men who were answering their country's call had touched every area of the country, and Darlington was no exception. The Grammar School itself had been affected when Mr Wood's successor as headmaster, Mr L W Taylor, volunteered for the forces in 1914, becoming a captain in the Durham Light Infantry. He was wounded and taken prisoner, and did not return to the school until after the war ended in 1919. Mr A J Smith, the Classics master, acted as head in his absence.

The Creek household must have been one among tens of thousands who were extremely anxious about what the future would hold for their sons. Fortunately Norman was too young to be among the vast numbers of volunteers who enlisted on the great wave of patriotism that had swept through the country. The popularly-held belief at that time was that the war would be short and people were assuring each other "our brave lads will be home in a matter of months". But over-optimistic official communiqués and newspaper accounts couldn't hide for long the speed at which casualties were mounting. After two years of war the numbers of those killed, wounded or missing in action, together with the fact that fewer volunteers were coming forward, meant that to fill the ranks it was necessary in 1916 to bring in conscription. At first the relevant Military Service Act stated that all unmarried and able-bodied men between the ages of 19 and 39 had to enlist (Norman at that time was 18). But the dreadful toll of the war continued to deplete troop numbers, and within a few months the lower age limit had been reduced to 18. Norman's involvement in the war was therefore inevitable, although not immediate, as students in their final year in the sixth form were allowed to complete that year of study, and so be more qualified and mature to enable them to "take on the role of 2nd Lieutenants and be able to command men in battle".

At the end of his school career, now aged eighteen years and six months, Norman enlisted at the office in Larchfield Road, Darlington, and was drafted into the 5th Battalion of the Durham Light Infantry. After initial training, he was commissioned as a Second Lieutenant, "ready to lead men into battle".

CHAPTER TWO

THE FIRST WORLD WAR YEARS

1916-19

Enlistment, training, then embarkation, all in the space of a few months – this was what faced those conscripted in the autumn of 1916. The war situation in France and Belgium demanded it, and as a result, young men, many, like Norman, straight from school, found themselves thrust into the horrors of life and death on the battlefields of the Western Front.

Norman went with the 5th Battalion of the Durham Light Infantry to Flanders in the early part of 1917, experiencing life in the trenches at first hand. Two newspaper cuttings describe one particular episode at that time:

We continue to work forward slowly on the W. and S. W. sides of Lens. Our advance in the neighbourhood of Fontaine-les-

Croisilles on Monday night seems to have been particularly clean and successful though on a small scale. The troops engaged were chiefly Durham men. They went over at midnight, the objectives to be taken being a certain piece of rising ground and fortified road, with contiguous trenches, just north of Fontaine. Everything was carried without a hitch. The positions were found strongly held, and the casualties inflicted on the enemy seem to have been unusually heavy for the size of the operation. The Germans made counter-attack after counter-attack. All have so far been beaten off.

British Official General Headquarters, Tuesday.

Further information regarding the operation carried out by us last night N.W. of Fontaine-les-Croisilles shows that all our objectives were gained with little loss and twenty seven prisoners were taken. Two hostile counter-attacks delivered in considerable strength were successfully driven off. During the day our progress S.W. of Lens has continued and our troops have extended their gains.

unattributed newspaper cutting

These reports, typical of the time, gave no hint of the conditions on the ground the troops had to contend with – flooded areas, deforested and churned-up land, craters caused by both Allied and German artillery shells and mines and everywhere mud, mud, mud. Above ground there was the noise of enemy bombardment, and the stench of the dead and dying blanketed everything.

Norman, who spoke little about his time on the battlefront, later confided in his son Carey, born nine years after the war ended, that he saw British planes flying over their lines and decided that that was where he wanted to be. As he told his son: "Facing danger and possible death on the ground without any control over events was too terrible to contemplate. At least those chaps in the air seemed to have some say in their own destiny".

Had he known then that the average life expectancy of aircrew was somewhere around four months, it might have given him some pause for thought. However, whether his assessment was accurate or not, he applied to transfer from the Durhams to The Royal Flying Corps. He chose the right moment to do so, although he would not have known this. From July to December 1916 four hundred RFC pilots and observers were reported killed or missing. To maintain aircrew numbers and to fulfil the dictum of Major General Trenchard, Commander of the RFC, that there should be 'no empty places in the mess rooms after missions', there was an increase in recruitment. Trainee pilots were ideally 'young men who could ride well, either a horse or a motorbike'.

At that time the Allies were using single-seat fighter aircraft, generally referred to as 'scouts', which were inferior in performance to the new German Albatross 111 'fighting scout', while the RFC's two-seater aircraft, used for surveillance and aerial spotting, were not suited to air-to-air combat. To rectify the situation the RFC was now being equipped with the De Havilland DH4 bomber, which was a great improvement on the Corps' BE 2e aircraft; in time it came to be widely regarded as the best reconnaissance bomber in the war. The BE 2e had a top speed of only 82 mph and a ceiling of 10,000 feet. Unable to outrun or outclimb enemy fighters it had become known among the flyers as 'Fokker fodder'. In comparison, the DH4, with a top speed of 117 mph and a ceiling of 16,000 feet, was a much more formidable machine. Its main drawback and greatest vulnerability was the location of the fuel tank between the two open cockpits. Because a number of them were hit by enemy aircraft fire and blew up in mid air, some flyers referred to the planes as 'flaming coffins'. However, in time, aircrew became more familiar with the DH4 and increasingly confident in its capabilities.

Norman's application for transfer having been successful, he returned from France in late August 1917, and on the 26th of that month he began training as an observer. The role of observer encompassed many skills that were new to him. As well as the experience of flying in an open cockpit biplane, he had to acquire the basic knowledge of handling the machine, in case the pilot became incapacitated. Other skills peculiar to the role of the observer were the assessment of the accuracy of ground artillery and relaying that information to commanders on the ground. The observers acted as 'the eyes of the gunners', an increasingly important task.

Bomb-aiming and the use of a heavy, unwieldy, hand-held camera to photograph any troop concentrations, gun batteries and ammunition dumps in enemy territory were additional skills to be learned. Perhaps most important of all in terms of self-preservation, an observer had to be constantly searching the skies for marauding enemy aircraft and be prepared to deal with an approach from the sides or rear of his plane, as the pilot had only a fixed, forward-facing machine gun. The observer had a swivel-mounted Lewis gun.

Trainee observers like Norman, who had been in the infantry, were familiar with the Lewis gun, but firing it and, if necessary, partly stripping it to free a jammed barrel in flight, was vastly different in the air compared with on the ground. The cramped space in the observer's cockpit meant there was a real danger of losing a vital piece over the side, and the thought of this must have added to the pressure. There was a great deal to be learned in a short space of time.

The RFC Machine Gun School had been based at Dymchurch (also known as Hythe or Pelmarsh) since 1915, with the aircraft based at nearby Lympne airfield. However, early in 1917 a new airfield was constructed at Dymchurch and the school was renamed No.1 (Auxiliary) School of Aerial Gunnery. As well as new hangars there were new accommodation huts, but the increased numbers on the courses left them unable to meet the demand. Consequently part of the Imperial Hotel in Hythe was requisitioned. This was a luxurious hotel, formerly catering for well-heeled holiday makers, so for the six weeks of the course Norman and the other ex-Flanders men who were billeted there must have thought they were living in a dream world compared to the trenches they had left behind.

Besides lectures and practical mock-ups, the trainees put in around 12 hours flying time in RE7 bombers, which had been used in France until they were withdrawn in August 1916 and used in training establishments in England.

After successful completion of that course, Norman had two weeks' leave back home in Darlington before joining his first squadron, No. 62, based at Cirencester in Gloucestershire. There he gained experience in another aircraft, the Bristol Fighter, a plane which became one of the most successful in the war.

However, the weeks spent at Hythe and Cirencester were simply a prelude to the serious, dangerous work which lay ahead in France. In November Norman received his posting as a fully qualified Observer to No. 25 Squadron, which was based at Boisdinghem, eight miles due west of St Omer in North West France. Accommodation was not up to Imperial Hotel standard, but it was a great deal better than in the trenches – weatherproof huts made of a wooden frame covered with heavy canvas. These were portable and so moved with the squadron when circumstances determined a retreat or advance.

Only the previous month the squadron had been

moved from the 10th Army Wing to the 9th and was now covering all the British Army fronts. Long-range reconnaissance, photography and bombing of distant targets in formations protected by Bristol escort fighters was now their daily work. A hectic time lay ahead for Norman. He must have been delighted to find the squadron was well equipped for the task with DH4 bombers.

His first flight on 12th November 1917, with a Lt. Ross as pilot, is recorded in his flying log as a 35-minute test flight around the airfield. Whether this was to familiarise him with the area or with the plane, or for Lt. Ross to assess the squadron's newest observer, is a matter of conjecture. Norman's next six hours of flying time, spread over two weeks because of bad weather conditions, were used to practise photography with the heavy hand-held camera. He flew with four different pilots (Lieutenants Pohlmann, Wensley, Pugh, and Captain Pearce), so he was being fairly quickly incorporated into the squadron's aircrew fraternity.

The real 'war in the air' started for him on the 30th November, with a bombing raid on Oisy-le-Vergen, north of Cambrai. This was a low level (3000 feet) two-hour flight taking them into German-held territory to drop the two 230lb bombs the plane carried. Norman, as observer, acted as bomb aimer. It is not difficult to imagine how he must have felt this first time – probably a mixture of exhilaration and the desire to get back safely to their airfield, followed by satisfaction with a job carried out as he'd been trained to do.

In December 1917 and January 1918 Norman flew 24 operational missions. These involved bombing raids on aerodromes and railway stations, with aerial photography when possible, as the weather at the turn of the year, with low cloud and fog in river valleys, resulted in many 'wash-outs' as far as photographs were concerned. Very soon this must have been looked upon as the normal day's work, but the flying log mentions occasions when flights did not go according to plan, such as this one:

3rd December. Machine DH4 No. C 7609 Pilot Lt. Pohlmann Bombing raid. Target - Crevecoeur (South of Cambrai). Forced landing at Belle Vue airfield.

This was on the return leg of the flight, and the forced landing was due to engine trouble which necessitated an overnight stop for repairs. As winters in that area were often severe, the problem was probably due to very low temperatures affecting the oil in the sump and causing a bearing to seize up. Belle Vue was only 30 miles from Boisdinghem, and they flew back to base the following morning.

4th January Machine DH4 No. A 2145 Pilot Lt. Tate Photography re. troop and munition movements. Target – Valenciennes. Landed near Amiens for more petrol.

This had been a long four-hour flight, but fortunately Bertangles, where they landed, was back behind Allied lines, and with more fuel on board they reached their base 55 minutes later.

30th January. Machine DH4 No. C 7605 Pilot Lt.

Pohlmann Photography of aerodromes. Target – St Amand, Valenciennes. Forced landing in field near home base.

From a flying point of view this was probably the most frightening experience. The engine cut out shortly after take-off after they had set course for their target. However, from a height of only 250 feet, a successful forced landing was made. Both Pohlmann and Norman must have thanked their lucky stars that there was little or no wind that morning. Had there been one, the prospect of turning into it for landing, without power and insufficient height, and with a full tank of petrol, would not have borne thinking about. Fortunately, not only were the two of them able to walk away from the aircraft but the plane itself was flying again two days later.

By now some of the flights were deep behind enemy lines, and to avoid German fighters they were flying at their 16,000 feet ceiling. Thigh-length flying boots were an essential part of their kit, but the cold was a problem not just for the flyers but for their equipment, the Lewis gun in particular having a disturbing tendency to jam at very low temperatures. Additionally, the lack of oxygen in the thin air reduced their ability to operate effectively. On one occasion, having managed to reach a height of 18,400 feet, Norman records in his flying log that he had fainted before recovering in time to take photographs of the Laon area.

On the 3rd March the squadron moved from Boisdinghem to Serny. The date was to be implanted in Norman's memory. He flew to their new base with Lt.

Pohlmann in DH4 No. C 7605. In the previous three weeks they had flown seven missions together in that plane, five of them over enemy territory, and spent a total of fifteen hours in the air, but this was to be their last flight together. Norman returned to England the next day for an eight-day course in wireless telegraphy.

Two years after the start of the war Major General Trenchard had realised that for aerial observation work to be most useful to troops on the ground a better, quicker form of communication needed to be developed. Biggin Hill, a name which would be forever linked with the Battle of Britain in the Second World War, had been chosen as the site of an aerodrome where research scientists could develop and test equipment, and in July 1917 a workable system was devised. As Germany had not yet produced such a system this gave the Allies a slight advantage. However, the RFC observers needed to be trained in its use, so a School of Wireless Telephony was established at the aerodrome for that purpose. Groups of observers were brought back from their squadrons in France for the eight-day course, which involved intensive theory work as well as practical tests in the air.

At the end of the course Norman returned to his squadron in France to be informed that Lt. Pohlmann, with Lt. Roy Ireland as his observer, had been shot down on the next mission after his last with Norman, and both men had been killed. This must have been an awful blow, as they had flown so many times together, and in that aircraft. All aircrew were aware of the falling survival rates, due largely to German improvements in aeroplane weaponry, but this tragedy must have brought it home with chilling effect.

However, Norman was given little time to reflect or grieve, as the day after his return he was flying, this time with Lt. Lindley, on two aerial photographic missions over La Fere and Laon, with a total flying time of six and a half hours. On the first of them they were attacked by seven German planes. Despite their Bristol fighter escort, they were driven off and had to return to base. Later in the day the mission was repeated and this time they were successful, with 15 photographs taken.

Two days later more missions to the same area, this time with Lt. Wensley, resulted in another 18 photographs. This area was coming under increasing scrutiny by both British and French reconnaissance aircraft, as it was thought to be the location of heavy German artillery. However, the importance of the Laon Corner, as it came to be known, increased enormously on 23rd March when shells fell on Paris. At first they were thought to be bombs dropped by planes, but when it was established that no planes had flown over the city that morning the French authorities reluctantly had to come to the conclusion that German scientists and engineers had produced a gun capable of firing shells a distance of at least 75 miles. This was more than twice the distance ever achieved before, and far exceeded the renowned 'Big Bertha' gun the Germans had used in 1914.

The blow to French morale which this

bombardment caused in that last week in March resulted in a frantic search for the location of the 'Paris Gun'. The nearest suitable point of the German lines was in the Crépy Forest area in the Laon Corner. All available aerial photographs would have been pored over in this search, and those taken by Norman and his fellow observers must have formed part of the evidence.

This was particularly dangerous work. To minimise the chances of being hit by anti-aircraft fire or attracting the attention of enemy aircraft, the pilot had to change direction every 15 to 20 seconds, yet maintaining a constant height and a straight course was best for good photographs. The aerial photographic work by both English and French flyers was crucial in pinpointing the target. French artillery gunners silenced the Paris Gun for at least a month. The effect of the shelling of Paris and, therefore the importance of finding 'Long Bertha' (the German name for the gun), was detailed in Henry W. Miller's book, *The Paris Gun*.

The involvement of Norman, although not mentioned in the book (none of the flyers were), can be judged from the fact that when it was published in 1930 his wife, Lilian, bought a copy and gave it to him. By chance that same book, eighty years later, was given to Norman's grandson. As well as containing Norman's Ex Libris sticker it is inscribed 'Norman 1930 from Wiggy' (Lilian's nickname within the family). Several newspaper cuttings relating to German long-range guns were found inside the book, as well as an aerial photograph 'taken by a British observer'.

On the 6th March the squadron moved again to Villers-Bretonneux, ten miles east of Amiens, but not before Norman and Lt. Wensley were credited with shooting down a German Albatross plane on the 18th February while on a photographic mission over the Laon Corner. Here is the official report:

"While taking photographs of POUILLY at about 12.30 pm, we were attacked by three enemy scouts (probably Albatross). On firing at them they broke formation and dived down. Just afterwards, a single-seater scout of the Nieuport type, climbing rapidly, attempted to attack us, by getting on our tail. Lieut. Wensley dived on him from close range and the E. A. immediately stalled, giving the observer, 2/Lt. Creek, an easy close-range shot. After a long burst by 2/Lt. Creek E. A. toppled over on one wing and went down in a spin and was last seen by observer about 1,000 feet from the ground, still out of control."

The war continued to escalate. Although aerial photography continued to be an important element of the squadron's work, bombing was beginning to feature more and more. At first the targets were mainly aerodromes and railway sidings, and these involved formations of up to ten DH4s with fighter escorts. But on the ground the Germans were about to mount what would be their last big offensive. With the collapse of the Russians on the Eastern Front due to the revolution of 1917, the German troops were being brought from there to increase strength in Flanders. The British troops, already depleted and with few reinforcements available, were now attempting to hold a line of 145 miles. They were in a desperate situation and after the 24th March they had to give ground almost daily.

The last week in March also witnessed a great increase in the numbers of aircraft, both Allied and German, being used in support of their ground troops, and RFC losses of machines and aircrew were extremely heavy. Many years later, when asked by a grandson how the British had won when the Germans had so many planes, Norman thought for a moment, then answered with one word, "spirit".

At the time Villers-Bretonneux was being heavily bombarded as the Germans were pushing towards Amiens, and it was necessary for 25 squadron to move once more, as there was a danger of their airfield being overrun. They moved to Beauvois near St Pol, where Nos. 27 and 79 squadrons were already stationed. Two days after this move official word came through to Major Duffus, the Commanding Officer of the squadron, that Norman had been awarded the Military Cross. The citation for the award was later issued in the Supplement to the London Gazette No. 5693 dated 13th May 1918. His citation reads:

For conspicuous gallantry and devotion to duty. He carried out several successful reconnaissance of enemy aerodromes and railways, and obtained valuable information often under the most difficult weather conditions. On one occasion he took several photographs of an enemy aerodrome though he was attacked by an enemy machine and subjected to anti-aircraft fire. He displayed the greatest skill and determination.

Whether there would have been much of a celebration is doubtful, as the following day Norman's log shows that he was on two bombing missions on railway sidings and on towns which the Germans had occupied in their late March advance. These included Cambrai, Troye, Noyon and Albert. Cambrai was a particularly important target, as it was a railhead and junction for supplying the German Armies on the Western Front.

An example of his brief, almost laconic, log entries very much understates these missions:

7.4.18
Cambrai. Bombing. Leader in 6 Formation.
Much anti-aircraft fire and 5 enemy aircraft.

It was about this time that a new element was introduced into the role of the Allied bombers – the low level machine-gunning or 'strafing' of transport and troop columns. As well as the swivel-mounted Lewis machine gun operated by the observer, the pilot now had a Vickers machine gun synchronised with the propeller's rotation. With these armaments a great deal of havoc could be inflicted among convoys, with many casualties. Norman would almost certainly have experienced mixed emotions with this role, having been an infantry man himself in his early days.

28.3.18
Ablancourt. Bombing. Low strafing, 500 rounds on roads.

29.3.18
Fresnoy. Bombing. Low strafing, good hits on troops.

The squadron was moved again on the 29th March, this time to Ruisseauville, well back from the front line on the ground. From there they continued with long-range, high-altitude bombing and photographic raids which took them up to 100 miles into enemy territory. For Norman the two weeks from the 24th March to the 7th April saw him go out on eight bombing missions. The strain on a young man just past his twentieth birthday must have been immense. An analysis of his flying log reveals that from mid November 1917, when he joined 25 squadron in France, to late April 1918 he flew on 62 missions, 48 of them into enemy territory. The only breaks he had in that time were the eight-day wireless telegraphy course at Biggin Hill and the occasions when the weather was impossible to fly in. He saw six months of flying action of various kinds with a total flying time of 125 hours 40 minutes. It was now more than time for him to pass on his experience to trainee observers at a training establishment in England, and at the same time recharge his batteries.

Meanwhile the tide of the war was turning on the ground on the Western Front as the German offensive slowly ground to a halt due to rain, difficulties with their supply trains and the reinforcing of Allied forces with American troops. The German retreat started, and 25 squadron were heavily involved in aerial reconnaissance of the areas the advancing troops were retaking. With Germany's surrender on the 11th November 1918, Norman's active combat role was at an end. However, his involvement with 25 squadron was to continue until July 1919. His flying log shows that in early 1919 he was at Cranwell in Lincolnshire as a pilot under instruction flying an Avro 504 bi-plane. All the flights were at less than 4000 feet and under an hour's duration – a far cry from what he had been used to in France, and without the distractions of enemy aircraft or anti-aircraft fire.

His comments in the 'remarks' column of the log give just a hint of the enjoyment these flights gave him: 'Joy-ride in Avro', 'Turns and side-slips', 'First long flight and some stall turns'. And finally in another aircraft: 'First flip in a Handley Page'.

Norman wasn't finished with serious flying, as June 1919 saw him back with his squadron based in Cologne, Germany as part of the Allied Army of Occupation. Their trusty DH4s had now been largely replaced by DH9A aircraft. Probably the major difference as far as Norman was concerned was that the pilot's and observer's cockpits were closer together and that, plus better wireless equipment, meant closer collaboration was possible. The squadron's role was one of observing that the conditions laid out for the defeated German Army and Air Force were adhered to.

Norman's log reflects this, with almost all of the flights being aerial photography of the Rhine valley and towns of the Ruhr, the former powerhouse of German armaments. Log entries read: 'Course Cologne to Bonn. 18 overlaps of the Rhine – O.K.' and 'Course Cologne, Düsseldorf etc. 7 pinpoint photos. – O.K.'

Somehow, during the summer of 1919, perhaps as an attempt to return to peace-time pursuits, some cricket matches had been played by various Army and RAF units. Norman had played in several, and to such good effect that he was selected for the RAF v The Army for a two-day match at the Oval test ground in London. He more than justified his place in the side by achieving the best bowling analysis and scoring a century in the second innings.

However, although peace-time and leisure pursuits were welcomed with open arms, for many flyers and their ground crews this was an uncertain time. At the end of the war the RAF had almost a quarter of a million officers and men. Only for some of them could a continuing career in the service be a possibility. Others perhaps hoped they might be taken on by the companies entering the commercial airline field, who were at first using converted bombers such as the De Havillands. This latter could have been a possible route for Norman, especially with his recent trainee pilot's course at Cranwell, but he had already decided his future lay in medicine. With that in mind he left the service and enrolled as a student at Trinity College, Cambridge on 1st of October 1919.

Back home in Darlington, in the period between leaving the RAF and starting his studies at Cambridge, Norman learned the sad news that two of his grammar school friends had been killed while serving as aircrew. John Worstenholm was a pilot with the RFC and Harold Easby an observer with the Royal Naval Air Service. If any further evidence was needed to convince Norman that he was fortunate to have survived the previous three years, this must surely have been it.

CAMBRIDGE

1919-1921

Travelling by train from Darlington to Cambridge in October 1919, Norman had plenty of time to cast his mind back over his experiences of the previous three years. Like so many other eighteen-year-olds during the Great War, he had been forced to accept a role he almost certainly wouldn't have chosen. Now, having been one of the fortunate ones to come through the conflict unscathed, he was about to take the first step on the road to a professional career.

Much as he must have wanted to get on with the necessary training for his peace-time life, he may well have wondered how he would cope with the return to a scholar's role, and with the more demanding academic work involved. He was now twenty-one, and the only books he had opened in the recent past had been flying and wireless telegraphy manuals. On that train journey he must have been filled with a mixture of excitement and concern. But in typical fashion he was determined to see it through.

To say that Trinity College and Cambridge were a different world from the one Norman had known would be a massive understatement. Darlington, despite links with the Quaker movement, involvement with early railways, and his attendance at a grammar school with some history, couldn't remotely compare with the famous Fenland town, which had a renowned academic tradition going back several centuries.

Trinity itself, although not the oldest of the colleges, was founded by Henry VIII in 1546. While there had been highs and lows in the College's history, Norman couldn't fail to be impressed, if not overawed, by some of the luminaries who had been students there; foremost among them being Isaac Newton. However, to quote from G M Trevelyan's *Historical Sketch* of the college: 'During the four years of World War One, undergraduate life had almost come to an end due to potential students and many of the younger academic staff enlisting'. Trevelyan likened the return of life and youth to the college to a flood.

On October 1st 1919 Norman was part of that flood, although, despite his war record, he would have been the first to admit that there were others who received more attention, such as Prince Albert (who later became King George VI) and his brother Prince Henry (later Duke of Gloucester). Throughout his life Norman was a staunch supporter of the royal family, so he must have felt some pride at sharing his undergraduate time with the sons of the monarch.

As the number of first-year students in the college was just over two hundred, the atmosphere and mingling which would have taken place was village-like. Some of the students were straight from their grammar school studies and many from public schools, as Trinity had always had close links with Winchester, Eton, Harrow and so on, while others, such as Norman, came from active service in the forces. Norman entered the college as a 'pensioner', that is a fee- paying student.

Returning servicemen were given the option to condense their degree course from three years (nine terms) to two years (six terms) to enable them to start their civilian careers as soon as possible. To do this they had to spend a full two years at college without taking the long vacations, and to obtain their degrees they had to pass the same examinations as the three-year students.

Norman had intended to study medicine, but in the second term he switched to the Natural Sciences degree course. Family anecdote suggests that he changed from medicine because he found the sight of blood disturbing. Possibly he was influenced by a more pragmatic factor – the medical degree was lengthy and would require more funds than the Natural Sciences degree, which could be completed under the shortened course option. Whichever of these reasons is correct,

Norman changed his academic course and also his career aim. He decided that teaching was to be the career for him and he aimed to be on that professional ladder after his time at Trinity. By then he would be twenty-three years old.

Almost before his academic work started in earnest, Norman was back in uniform, but this time only for a day. On the 19th October he had received a telegram requesting his attendance at Buckingham Palace to receive his Military Cross. His mother and father travelled from Darlington to be present at the ceremony. It must have been a very proud moment for them, and no doubt it brought back memories of how worried they had been about Norman's safety during the war.

Norman was serious about his studies, but as always in his adult years, he found time to devote to sport. In common with all the Cambridge colleges before the war, Trinity had a history of sporting achievement, but post-war it was most fortunate in that its Master from 1918 to 1940 was Sir Joseph John Thomson. JJ, as he was affectionately known, took a keen interest in the college's sporting performances. Norman would very quickly have come to his notice, as he was chosen to play for the university football team against Oxford University at the Queen's Club ground, West Kensington in the December of his first term, following an injury to another player. This led to his being awarded a much coveted 'Blue'. The game ended in a 2-2 draw.

Norman missed the Varsity match in 1920 as he himself was injured, but gained his second football 'Blue' in December1921. Unfortunately Cambridge lost the match, played at Chelsea's Stamford Bridge ground, 3-0. It was perhaps of little consolation to Norman and the rest of the team to read in the match report:

The match was a thoroughly sporting contest, perfectly delightful because of the spirit in which it was played. I have read how, in the olden times, football was played without a referee. There might as well have been no referee today as he hardly ever sounded his whistle. The theory, of course, was that twenty-two gentlemen were playing the game, and it was a matter of honour that not one of them should commit a wilfully wicked act or do a dirty trick. This was the real sport of football – glorious, exhilarating, exciting, and, in fact, one of the best Varsity matches seen for years.

This way of conducting oneself on a football field was very much in line with Norman's personal view and was perhaps one reason why he remained an amateur player all his career and why he was happy playing for the Corinthian football team after he left Cambridge, despite several professional teams being keen to sign him.

Life at Cambridge had its bizarre moments. During his second term Norman's rooms at Trinity were broken into and various articles stolen. These included a box of dissecting instruments and two books, Keith's *Vertebrate Embryology and Morphology* and Borradaile's *Manual of Zoology*. Two days after reporting the loss Norman called in to Heffer and Son's bookshop in Cambridge to replace them and was offered the very copies he had previously owned. It transpired that a student at Caius College had sold them to the shop and also offered for sale a box of dissecting instruments.

Norman had to attend the next Cambridge Borough Quarter Sessions as a formal witness. Evidence was produced to show that the same young man had stolen items from the University library and the Archaeological Museum. In mitigation the accused's solicitor stated that his client's war service in France had aggravated a long standing kleptomanic condition. Norman probably had mixed feelings about such a defence, having seen so many of his comrades overcoming the trials of war.

Annoying though this episode was, it was a minor one; his Trinity time was devoted to study and to sport. His sporting prowess wasn't just evident on the football field but extended to athletics. Besides helping Trinity to win the Cambridge Inter-Collegiate Football Cup in the 1920-21 season, he was a member of the team which won the Inter Collegiate Athletics Cup in 1921. Norman was a sprinter and, as well as taking part in official inter-college competition, he almost certainly would have attempted the traditional annual Trinity Great Court Run, which takes place at noon on Matriculation Dinner Day. (This run gained wider prominence in 1981 when it featured in the major Oscar winning film 'Chariots of Fire').

The Great Court is four-sided and the distance around it is approximately 370 metres. The aim of a runner is to complete the cobbled circuit in less time than it takes the college clock to strike the hour of 12 (noon). As the clock, since it was first put up in 1726, has always struck the preparatory chimes of four quarters and then two sets of twelve, the total time is between 43 and 44.5 seconds, depending on how recently the mechanism has been wound. At the time of Norman's run this feat had never been achieved, a situation which did not change until 1927, when Lord Burghley finally managed it (the following year Burghley won the 400 metres hurdles at the Olympic Games in Amsterdam).

Although Norman, with his competitive spirit, would have been disappointed not to beat the chimes, he must have taken some consolation from the fact that the captain of the Trinity athletics team also failed. This man was Guy Montagu Butler, who in 1919 was the British Amateur Athletic Association 440 yards champion. In the 1920 Antwerp and 1924 Paris Olympic Games he won four medals. It was not until 2007 that the second successful run was achieved, by Sam Dobin, a 2nd year Economics student.

Although the compression of Norman's course to two years (six terms) meant that Norman was unable to enjoy the luxury of the long vacations, these two years were not restricted to study and sport. There was also time for socialising. In this respect, chance was to play a major role. In the few months he had been in Flanders serving with the Durham Light Infantry he had 'palled up' with a chap from Cambridge called Albert Booth. However, with Norman transferring to the RFC and the difficulties of keeping in touch in wartime, their friendship appears to have foundered. Norman still had Albert's address, and not knowing if he had survived the war he wrote a letter more in hope than expectation.

Albert was home, fit and well, and he invited Norman to a family gathering at the Booth home. There he met Albert's sister, Lilian, who worked in Cambridge as secretary to the owner of a horticultural business. From that first meeting their friendship developed.

During the 1920 Michaelmas period break Norman was back home in Darlington. On Christmas Day and Boxing Day he was playing in mixed hockey matches in the grounds of the home of Mr and Mrs. A E Lockey at Middleton St George. The weather was unseasonably mild; according to the newspaper report of the proceedings it seems to have been a most enjoyable two days when 'Mrs. Lockey, with her usual kindly thought, provided most acceptable liquid refreshment and fruit for the participants in the games'.

That one sentence seems to capture the very essence of a carefree, peaceful England. Of more long-term significance for Norman was that one of the other players was Lilian Booth, who was listed as being from Cambridge. One assumes that she and Norman had travelled up to County Durham together and that she would have met Norman's parents and brothers on that visit.

Lilian obviously made an impact on the hockey field, as the same newspaper report shows:

The player who caught the eye more than any other by reason of her delightfully refreshing exposition of how the game should be played was the dainty little lady from Cambridge. On more than one occasion an opponent was heard to call to her, "Well played little 'un". A term of endearment not frequently heard at Middleton.

Could that have been Norman calling out encouragement to her? I like to think so. For Norman, social hockey such as this was a pleasant diversion from his football and athletics exploits. So too was tennis. In this sporting area, although he had talent, pressure of time meant that he could only ever be an occasional player. In spite of that, he reached the final of the autumn lawn tennis tournament at Scarborough in 1921. His hand/eye coordination and his speed and balance round the court made him a worthy finalist. In a close-fought three-set match he was eventually beaten by the Yorkshire champion, Mr D Hick, 6-4, 4-6, 6-4.

Even at this time in Norman's life it was being noticed that somehow he was managing to cram more into it than others. A humorous, anonymous entry in a magazine at the time stated: 'Creek, F N S: Motto; 'Every minute tells'. Dangerous when disturbed or teased. At home Bank Holidays from 11.05 to 11.10 pm. No admission except on business. Visitors are advised to obtain written permit beforehand. Can quote answers to all Natural Science Tripos papers since 1818. Would be glad of suggestions for 1922. Will probably play 'soccer' for Europe v. America if time can be arranged. Refuses to buy this magazine!'

At the end of the autumn term 1921, on the completion of a very full two years at Cambridge and now armed with his Bachelor of Arts degree, it was time for Norman to seek a teaching position.

For the rest of his life Norman looked back on his time at Cambridge with great fondness and was delighted when some thirty years later his son, Carey, also become a Trinity College student. Norman had made a number of real friends there. Of his fellow Trinity students, he was very happy in the company of Guy Butler, the Ashton brothers (particularly Hubert), John Morrison and Carey Francis. Another life-long friend was Graham Doggart, a fellow County Durham man, although a student of King's College. But the most significant friendship of all was with Lilian, who in 1924 became his wife.

DAUNTSEY'S

1923-1954

For three years, mainly in his late teens, Norman's course in life had been dictated for him. He had been actively involved in a war in which danger and excitement in equal measure were almost a daily occurrence. This had been followed by an equally full two years in the setting of an august Cambridge college, involving intense academic study and athletic performance. At the age of twenty three he had a Military Cross, a Cambridge degree, a football 'Blue' and an England amateur international football cap. He planned to teach, but a career in football must have been tempting.

If the decision had been left to the sports writers in the popular press, he would have signed for one of the professional teams which had been alerted to his goal-scoring abilities. Only five feet eight inches in height and ten stone in weight, he was not considered by opposing centre halves to be much of a threat - until the ball came his way, when his speed and close control confounded them. He was already being touted as the solution to the centre forward problem in England's full international team.

Norman must have been well aware of his prospects, as he had already played, with some success, with and against professionals while in the forces. He had also played twice for his home town team of Darlington in Third Division League games, to such good effect that they were bitterly disappointed that they could not call upon him for their Easter 1921 fixtures, as he had already committed to the Corinthians tour to Denmark and Holland. He was a football and fitness fanatic and it must have been very difficult to turn away from a life as a professional sportsman.

He did not choose that path, for three reasons. Firstly, he was an amateur sportsman through and through; the notion of winning at all costs was anathema to him. The ethos of the Corinthian Football Club, incorporating sportsmanship, fair play, playing for the love of the game and having respect for your opponents and the officials, suited him perfectly. (Although when he was asked if he would have agreed with the earliest Corinth players who, if an opponent was sent off the field, took one of their own players off to avoid having an advantage, he smiled and said, "I think that might have undermined the authority of the referee".)

Secondly, he wanted to be a member of a profession which would give him an opportunity to work with young people and promote the values he held to be important. Thirdly, professional footballers were not well paid in those days and their career could be very short. As a schoolmaster he could have a lifelong, reasonably paid, career which would allow him to actively pursue his own football, and later cricket, interests.

Norman's first teaching post was as Science Master at St Andrew's School in Eastbourne. He was only there for a year before he moved to Dauntsey's School in Wiltshire for the start of the autumn term 1923. Why he made the move is not readily apparent, but it could have been down to a combination of factors. In 1922 he had won his first amateur international football cap for England (he scored four goals in a 7-4 win against Wales) and had also started to play for the Corinthian team, which may have resulted in time away from the classroom. Indeed he had to be given leave of absence by the school to answer an urgent request by the Corinthians to bolster their team when they were on a tour of Holland; he only managed to get back in time by catching an Imperial Airways flight from Amsterdam to Croydon. He also had some sporting colleagues who were living in Wiltshire.

Another possible reason, perhaps even the main one, was that he was 'headhunted' by Dauntsey's. This school, in West Lavington on the edge of Salisbury

Plain, is now a highly respected public school. Dauntsey's was founded in 1542 as a boys' grammar school with money from the Mercers' Company in London, but it had had something of a chequered career up to the end of the First World War. The school history shows that in 1832 it had only one schoolmaster, who taught Religious Knowledge, with other subjects 'taught' by a twelve-year-old boy! As the owners of the estate who appointed the master specified that schoolwork should not interfere too much with farm work, the average leaving age was just over nine years!

The leaving age had increased to just over 12 by 1859, when the staff consisted of a master who was a clergyman and a certified schoolmaster as his assistant. However, in the 1870s, after a decade of decline, the school was considered by Her Majesty's Inspector to be 'of very doubtful benefit to the parish'.

Things did improve somewhat after that damning appraisal, but pupil numbers continued to fluctuate. The school was drifting, and needed a man of drive and vision to set it firmly on an upward course. In 1919 George Olive moved from Oundle School, where he had been Head of the Sixth Form, to become Headmaster at Dauntsey's, and he proved to be the man for the job. He set about transforming the school. As he told the governors, "It will not be cheap, school fees will have to rise, as I will be looking to attract the best staff".

In 1923 Norman Creek became one of George Olive's appointments. Norman certainly didn't come cheap. He and Lilian Booth (the 'little 'un' from the mixed hockey matches at Middleton St George) were planning to marry in the following April, so he accepted the job offer only on the proviso that the school would build a house for him and Lilian. This was agreed, and a small house was built in the school grounds next to the Ebenezer Chapel, ready for them to move into when they returned from their honeymoon in Switzerland at the end of the Easter break.

As one would expect, Norman threw himself wholeheartedly into the work and life of the school. Over the next few years, during the Easter holidays, accompanied by Lilian, he took groups of boys hiking and climbing in the Lake District. One of their favourite places was Skelwyth village and the nearby Falls, and they named their house Skelwyth.

At that time the school was called Dauntsey's Agricultural School and it had a small mixed farm, for practical training, attached to it. It provided mainly agriculturally-based education for a mixture of farm labourers' children, well- heeled gentlemen farmers' sons, and later, sons of commissioned officers in the Armed Forces. Most of the boys were boarders, among them Nigel Balchin, who became a popular novelist of the 1940s and 50s, and W Awdry, the creator of Thomas the Tank Engine. Awdry and his brothers had reason to remember Norman not only as one of their teachers but also because they later played some Minor Counties cricket matches for Wiltshire with him.

By 1930 the vision of George Olive and his governors (one of whom was H G Wells) was coming to fruition. The name was changed to Dauntsey's School and it was well set on the road to being a 20th century public school.

In 1928 Norman and Lilian's first child, Carey, was born. He was named after a close friend of Norman's from his Cambridge days, Carey Francis; the two of them had played in the Trinity football team. Growing up in the Skelwyth house must have been idyllic for Carey. He was shown how to milk a cow on the school farm, had rides on a wagon pulled by Prince, the farm horse, and with his father, he gave Prince handfuls of grass to eat in the field between Skelwyth house and the school playing fields.

Two years later, when Lilian was expecting again, she and Norman decided that the little house would be too small for the growing family. The school governors and the head agreed, and during the Easter holidays, while an extension was built, Norman, Lilian and three-year-old Carey stayed with the Olives in the headmaster's house. In 1931 Lilian gave birth to their second child, Heather.

In a very short space of time Norman had proved that George Olive had made a sound decision in bringing him onto the staff. As well as his personal qualities and his high profile as an international sportsman, his teaching expertise covered a good number of subjects, though Geography was his main responsibility and he taught that to Advanced Level.

He also coached the boys in a range of sports. At that time there was a need for improved sports facilities at the school and Norman organised and supervised the building of a squash court, tennis courts and the cricket scoreboard. As a good baritone, he was an active member of the school's Musical Society both as a choir member and soloist in the big concerts held at the end of each spring term. Further to all this, Norman was a lay reader, and he often took the service at the Little Cheverell church, which could just accommodate the eighty or so boarders at that time.

Perhaps his value to the school can be gauged by the fact that after only four years there he was responding for the school at The Old Dauntseians' Association meeting on behalf of the headmaster, who was unable to attend due to illness. With such wide-ranging skills and a genuine interest in the academic and social welfare of the boys, it is no surprise that Norman readily took on the role of housemaster. Being an integral part of a school that was year by year increasing in size and reputation was most satisfying, and he felt life for him and his family could hardly have been bettered.

However, during the latter part of the 1930s there was increasing concern throughout the country about the possibility of a new war. Norman must have been appalled at the thought that if such a conflict started, senior boys in the school would be thrust into the armed forces, much as he had been twenty-three years before, to face the horrors of war. However he was a pragmatist, and despite his deep reservations, he knew that if the worst happened he had to consider what role he might be able to take.

The outbreak of the Second World War in 1939 brought about several changes at the school. Land Army girls were now to be seen on the school farm. The farm itself proved very useful in times of shortages of food, as it was able to produce milk, eggs, vegetables and some fruit.

The staff and boys also played their part in the war effort. The Dauntseian magazine of March 1941 reported: "The School's contribution to the military situation has been the formation of a special Cyclist Section of the local Home Guard. Eighteen senior boys are involved and have been responsible for fire-watching on two nights a week and carry out drill and rifle firing on the local ranges in co-operation with the Devizes battalion". Also in that year, the Air Training Corps had been created nationally, with the aim of preparing cadets who might join the RAF or the Fleet Air Arm. It had been established by Royal Warrant, with King George VI as Air Commodore-in-Chief.

As Norman and two other masters, Mr Scott and Mr Horner, had been given RAF Voluntary Reserve commissions, an Air Training Corps was formed in the school, with seventy full cadets and a score of keen juniors. Parades were held every Wednesday afternoon and there were lectures, aircraft recognition groups, signalling and machine-gun practice. The Corps was affiliated to the local RAF aerodrome at Upavon, which had originally been the RAF's Central Flying School for the training of Flying Instructors. However, it had only grass runways, which could not cope with the larger, faster modern aircraft, so it had been downgraded as one of many Flying Training Schools for RAF aircrew. Nonetheless, for the Dauntsey's Cadet Force it was a great fillip to be closely associated with an historic and still active airfield.

A further advantage for the school cadets and for Norman was that from 1942 to 1944 the station's Commanding Officer was Group Captain A J Holmes. He and Norman had much in common – both had served as aircrew in the RFC in the First World War, and both were keen sportsmen. In the inter-war years Holmes had played cricket for Sussex, and in 1938-39 he had been manager of the MCC team which toured South Africa. The role Norman was seeking in the war effort probably resulted from this friendship when he was appointed liaison officer with this local station, and later his remit was extended to take in the whole of the South West of the country.

In 1943, Norman was awarded the MBE (Military Division) in the King's Birthday Honours List for this liaison work. This was the first honour to be given to the ATC. The investiture took place at Buckingham Palace on 15th February 1944 and King George VI presented the award. One can only speculate on the words exchanged between the two men, but perhaps there was some mention of their time together at Trinity College in 1920. On this occasion Norman's two guests at the ceremony were his wife, Lilian, and son Carey, who was now fifteen and was proudly wearing his ATC uniform as a member of the Dauntsey's Cadet Force.

In the years 1941 to 1945 Norman was working full-time as a teacher/housemaster as well as acting as liaison officer between the ATC and the RAF. His flying log shows that in that time he had seventy-one flights, totalling over sixty-six hours' flying time. Some of these involved visiting aerodromes in all parts of the country arranging camps, training, sporting activities, and flying experience for groups of cadets. Others were visiting airfields as part of his inspection duties and giving navigation lectures to trainee aircrew. He was also keen to maintain his own flying skills, and to familiarise himself with different, more modern, aircraft from those he had known in his WWI days he flew in nine different types.

A selection of entries taken from his flying log gives a picture of his work. Almost all the flights in the 1941 to 1943 period had a serious purpose, although there was the occasional light relief. However, by 1945 'tea and billiards at Overton Heath' after a flight from Norman's local aerodrome of Upavon gives more than a suggestion that the war was nearing its victorious conclusion.

FLYING LOG
Excerpts

14.8.41
Inspection at Sywell

16.8.41
Navigation Flight with Squadron Leader Orlinski, Chief Flying Instructor to Polish Forces in Britain.

17.8.41
First flight in a Miles Master. Touched 230 m.p.h.

7.6.42
Over Lavington to observe Home Guard exercise.

20.8.42
Brize Norton to Weston-on-the-Green in Airspeed Oxford to take Russian news correspondent to Upavon.

29.12.42
Avro Anson. Visit to Flying Training Command headquarters.

9.1.43
Inspecting Home Guard defences.

15.4.43
Upavon to Wittering. Conference lecture.

25.5.43
With F/L Booker, A.F.C. in Air Speed Oxford. Wizard low cross country. 170 miles at zero feet! (They were booked out to fly at 250 feet).

6-8 & 12.9.43
Bombing 'runs' over Sevenoaks Forest with 3 RAF personnel.

12.8.44
Upavon to Wyneswold for Loughborough Summer School course.

20.3.45
Upavon to Overton Heath and back in Air speed Oxford with F/L Hayter. Tea and billiards at Overton Heath.

During this time Norman had also been Assistant District Inspecting Officer to Admiral A V Campbell. In 1946, on the Admiral's retirement, he took over responsibility for the six corps in Wiltshire and was promoted to the rank of squadron leader. In that year he was awarded the Cadet Forces decoration. The presentation was made by Air Commodore le Croke at Dauntsey's. It was an honour which Norman was more than happy to share with the school. At the end of all this Norman and the others must have been most gratified to hear the Marshall of the RAF, Lord Portal, say, "In maintaining the flow of men to the RAF, the ATC made a decisive contribution towards victory".

THE FOOTBALL YEARS

1920-1936

The last chapter traced Norman's entry into the teaching profession and how, in a very short space of time, he became a valued member of staff at Dauntsey's School. He remained there until 1954. However, while teaching was his chosen profession and he gave it his all, sporting blood still ran in his veins. His own active participation in football, from 1920 to 1936, and cricket, from 1925 to 1954, was an important part of his life, so though largely concurrent with his teaching career, it is best dealt with in separate chapters.

The name of F N S Creek first appeared on the team sheet of the Corinthian Football Club on 31st January 1920. The game was against the First Division leaders, West Bromwich Albion, at their ground, The Hawthorns, in front of 15,000 spectators. The amateurs gave a good account of themselves, only losing by four goals to three. Norman would have felt quite at home in the team as Morrison, Hunter and Hubert Ashton had been his team-mates in the Varsity match against Oxford the previous month. It is highly probable that Ashton introduced Norman to the club, as they were both Trinity College men.

This was the first of Norman's 121 appearances for the club, mainly as centre forward. The only unusual aspect of this game was that Norman didn't find the net. In his other games for the club he scored 125 goals!

His second game, against Crystal Palace, then in the Southern League, also resulted in a 4-3 defeat, but Norman scored twice. In this match the old Corinthian ideals were illustrated when a penalty was awarded against them because a handball had prevented a certain goal from being scored. The goalkeeper, the Rev. B J Scott, moved to the side of his goal and the penalty taker was allowed to kick the ball into the unguarded goal!

A combination of injuries and the demands of his condensed course at Cambridge resulted in Norman missing the whole of the next football season. When he did return, his general all-round play, allied to his goal scoring ability, brought rave notices in the sporting press. The family press cuttings books include snippets which read: 'The finest amateur centre forward in the country is F N S Creek' and 'Creek is a good, fast, accomplished centre forward – a rarity these days'.

In 1922 he was selected for the amateur international match against Wales at Swansea. Although

Wales had won the previous year's encounter 2-0, this time they were no match for the English and lost 7-0. Norman scored four of the goals, a record for a player making his debut. The press cuttings album again:

Creek gave the most promising show as leader of the attack since the retirement of the great Vivian Woodward. He scored four goals – but it was not so much the number of times he netted the ball, and thus proved himself a strategic opportunist, as the manner in which he held the line throughout that stamped his play with the hallmark of excellence.

In these games, as with the Corinthian's games against other amateur sides, although they were played in a competitive spirit it was never to the detriment of fair play and sportsmanship. When the Corinthian club entered the Football Association Cup competition for the first time in the 1922/23 season they were drawn to play away against Brighton and Hove Albion, a professional team. It took the professionals three games to finally overcome the amateurs 1-0 after two 1-1 draws. The interest in how the Corinthians would fare is shown by the attendance figures: 25,000 at Brighton; 20,000 at the Crystal Palace ground for the first replay; 43,000 at Chelsea's Stamford Bridge ground for the second replay. Norman scored in the first game and so became the first Corinthian to score in an FA Cup match.

Although I am sure they would have liked to have won the tie, the club must have gained some consolation from the way their attitude to the game was appreciated by the crowd and by the referee. A local journalist reported:

The Corinthians and the referee between them turned it into one of the most unusual Cup ties I've ever watched. The Corinthians refused to be 'professional' in any of their methods (except in keenness) and followed their traditions. When Knight, right fullback, tipped a Brighton forward over, he picked him up, enquired after his health and gave him a friendly pat on the back. The crowd were highly amused and the referee, Mr Wildig, was most impressed. Politeness became the order of the day. A foul was later given against a Brighton back, to his annoyance, and he kicked the ball in among the crowd. Wildig made the player go and fetch the ball and hand it over politely to the Corinthian waiting for it. All this politeness did not stop it being a real 'willing' game. Nobody could complain that it was ladylike.

Some of the comments from the young ladies in the crowd must have caused blushes or burning ears among the Corinthian players, who in the main were fine-looking examples of young British manhood. Norman must have been embarrassed when, after he'd scored his goal, a young woman, bursting with excitement and delight, called out, "Ooh, isn't he just like the Prince of Wales!" He probably preferred that to the nickname of 'Hairpin' which had been given to him by the crowd at an international trial match at Bradford a few years earlier! Perhaps Fred May was influenced by that when he drew his caricature.

From 1921 the name of F N S Creek was rarely out

of the sports pages of the popular press. English football was desperately searching for a centre forward to replace the renowned Vivian Woodward, who had recently retired. Reporters vied with each other to be the first to recognise Norman's talent and many column inches were devoted to the cause. There were some doubters who considered him to be too slightly built for the job, but his supporters needed only to point to his almost uncanny knack of scoring goals against good quality, professional defenders. Those who were more analytical extolled his ball control, his all-round vision in leading the forward line, his opportunism in sight of goal and his speed. In his long career these skills remained intact, including his speed, even into his thirties.

In the early seasons of the 1920s the exploits of the Corinthians, and of F N S in particular, were not unnoticed by the members of the selection committee which was deliberating the line-up of the full international team to play France in Paris on May 10th 1923. To help them make their decision, a match was arranged between 'The North' and an England XI. F N S was chosen as centre forward for 'The North' because of his Darlington connection. As the *Sporting Life* reporter wrote:

This will be the severest test he has had. He will be up against Wilson of Sheffield Wednesday, the most scientific centre half in League football, and behind him are Clay (Tottenham Hotspur) and Lucas (Liverpool). If he comes out of this ordeal with credit he may prove to be the lineal successor to G O Smith and V J Woodward.

He obviously did come out of it with credit, for when the team of seven professionals and four amateurs was announced Norman was in his favoured position at centre forward. Alongside him, at inside right, was the captain of the side, Charles Buchan, the Sunderland (and later Arsenal) star. The game took place at the Pershing stadium in Vincennes on the outskirts of Paris. The stadium had been built by the US Military at the end of WWI and named after General Pershing, commander of American troops in France. It was opened in 1919, when it hosted the Inter-Allied Games, and then given to France by the USA.

For the England-France match there was a capacity crowd of 30,000. England played well, and despite having a man injured and finishing with ten men, they won 4-1, with Norman scoring in the 55th minute.

At this point in his football career Norman had an important decision to make. He had a full international cap, with the prospect of more, and there were a number of professional clubs keen to have him in their team. He must have been tempted, but as an idealist, he was influenced by the notion of how football, indeed any sport, should be played. For him the Corinthian spirit was all important.

J A H Catton, writing in *The Illustrated Sporting and Dramatic News*, summed up just what this spirit entailed: 'The Corinthians represent the spirit and art of amateurism in an era of professionalism. They play for love, not lucre. The ideal and realisable are nearly always conflicting in modern sport but the men of 'Corinth' have set the game above the prize, the match above the medal'.

As a result of this they did not enter a league but played friendlies, in some cases against professional teams who were more than willing to pit themselves and their reputations against the amateurs. For many years the only competition they entered was the annual Sheriff of London Shield, which was played for charitable causes. Later, in 1922-23, they entered the FA Cup competition, not to win at any cost but to showcase the quality of amateur football at its best. Norman was a firm believer in the value of football, played in a fair and proper manner, in helping peaceful international relations. He spoke and wrote on this theme in later years. So the fact that every year the Corinthians took the game (and the spirit) on foreign tours must have been another factor in his decision.

Norman's exploits on the football field continued to be widely reported. From the many games he played – over 100 for the Corinthians, seven England amateur internationals and many foreign tours (mainly in the Easter vacations from his duties at Dauntsey's) - I have chosen only a tiny selection. His home town team, Darlington, played in the Third Division North League and in 1923 while on vacation he was persuaded to turn out for them against Southport at the Feethams ground. He was accompanied by another Cambridge 'Blue' and County Durham man, A G Doggart, who much later was a member of the Football Association committee which appointed Alf Ramsey to the England manager's job.

The two of them, both forwards, transformed the Darlington side. The reporter in the local paper, writing under the by-line 'The Captain', stated:

Creek was as lively as a cricket. He did not score a goal, but he took so much watching that the others in the line had more ground than usual to work upon. Doggart too showed method in all he attempted and his finesse was great. If the two of them had been available for the past four weeks what a different outlook the Third North championship would have had. If their services are available over the Easter period then I think maximum points will be secured from Crewe Alexandra, Stockport and Walsall.

Unfortunately for The Quakers, both had committed themselves to the Corinthians' tour to Holland.

January 9th 1926 saw the 3rd round FA Cup tie between the Corinthians and Manchester City at the Crystal Palace ground. The game attracted a crowd of 30,000, who watched a thrilling 3-3 draw. Headlines in several newspapers give an indication of how the game went and to some extent where the sympathy of non-partisan reporters lay: 'Amateur forwards puzzle Manchester City'; 'Brilliant forward play against Manchester City'; 'Perplexed Pros'; 'Manchester saved by last minute effort'; 'Corinthians robbed of their reward'.

The game was played at a fast pace, and for over half an hour the Manchester defence was almost overwhelmed by the amateurs. In that time Norman scored the opening goal. Gradually the Manchester men settled and began to play to their First Division form and just before half time they equalised. It was feared that the amateurs would tire in the second half, and such fears seemed well founded when City scored a second goal. However, the Corinthians, though slowing, were far from finished and a cross shot from Hegan levelled things. Six minutes remained when Hegan provided a genuine cross this time and Norman turned it past Goodchild, the City keeper, to put them ahead.

A desperate Manchester threw everything into attack, but it looked increasingly likely that the Corinth men would triumph. There were only seconds remaining when Howard-Baker, the Corinthian goalkeeper, who had performed heroics in those dying minutes, was penalised for carrying the ball more than the six steps then allowed. When the referee blew his whistle for the infringement many in the crowd thought it was to end the game, with City beaten. However, it was a free kick and from it and the ensuing goalmouth melée the ball somehow found its way into the Corinthians' net. Manchester 'were mighty lucky to have forced a replay'.

The four days between that game and the replay, at Manchester's new, big Maine Road ground, was insufficient for the amateurs to recover from their exertions. Although they were only a goal down at half time they eventually lost 4-0.

The following season, 1926-27, the Corinthians were drawn to play Third Division side Walsall away in the 3rd round of the FA Cup. Walsall had been in good form in their recent matches and were especially at home on their sloping ground. A crowd of 16,600 turned up, more than their usual attendance, most expecting the professional side to win. The play during the first half seemed to confirm their opinion, as Walsall were much the better team. The Corinthians struggled to play their normal quick passing game. Only heroics by their defence, especially Howard-Baker, kept them in the game.

But this day fortune was on the side of the Corinthians, and just before the interval, in a rare attack, Norman scored. It was probably the 'softest' goal in his whole career, with a tame shot squirming through the arms of Wait, the Walsall keeper.

As occasionally happens in such matches the second half was a completely different story. The Corinthians found their true form and Walsall just fell away. Goals from Ashton (2) and Hegan completed what was almost a second half rout. Normally one would have expected Norman to have added more to his tally, but shortly after the opening goal he had fallen heavily and jarred his back. He finished the game, but only in a cautious fashion.

There were three weeks between the 3rd and 4th round ties, just time for Norman to recover, get back to peak fitness and resume playing. He must have been delighted, as the Corinthians had come out of the hat with the plum draw – Newcastle United, the leaders of the First Division, at the Crystal Palace ground. *The Times*, in its preview of the game, said: 'The Corinthians could not have been set a harder task. Newcastle United are probably the best team in the country'.

Because of the national interest in the match it was to be broadcast live by the BBC, only the second-ever broadcast match. It was also previewed in *Radio Times,* together with a diagram of a football pitch with numbered squares to help the commentators and their listeners.

January 29th 1927 was the great day. The weather conditions were better than expected and the pitch was fresh and green although very soft after overnight rain. Despite there being cup matches at West Ham, Fulham and Chelsea and the absence of many Millwall and Brentford supporters who had travelled to their away ties, by mid-morning thousands had entered the grounds of The Crystal Palace. Several trainloads of Newcastle supporters arrived at Kings Cross station from 5.30 am onwards, each man wearing a black and white rosette. According to an *Evening Standard* reporter they were all convinced the cup was already theirs. There was only one dissenting voice, heard to mutter, "even the best team can lose", and he was from Sunderland!

The supporters made their way to the Crystal Palace station. The Geordie fans spent the morning using pennies to start the models of fire engines, American locomotives, paddle steamers and many other mechanical devices housed in their glass cases under the great glass roof of the Palace. In the ground itself they were entertained by the band of the Irish Guards. It was a great day out, well worth the train fare and the cost, seven shillings and sixpence for a covered seat or three shillings and sixpence for a ring seat.

Over ten thousand tickets had been sold a week before the match and all seats had been taken up by the morning of the match. These ticket holders were allowed into the ground at 11 am and those paying at the turnstiles, for the standing areas, at noon. Estimates for the attendance vary from 56,000 to 80,000.

The teams arrived in charabancs shortly before one o'clock and tumultuous cheering greeted them when they came out to inspect the pitch before the scheduled 3 pm kick off. Unfortunately, the day before the game the Corinthians had had to radically alter their forward line. Due to a family bereavement F Hartley, the inside left, was unable to play, and A E Taylor, a right winger, was brought in. The rearrangement necessary to accommodate him meant that Norman was moved from centre forward to inside right. Although no match on paper for the full-time Newcastle team, which contained many international players, including the renowned Hughie Gallagher, the first half belonged mainly to the amateurs. Probably to the astonishment of most in the ground, they took the lead when a shot from Ashton finished off a move which had been started by 'an adroit pass by Creek' according to the *Daily Mail*. They held this lead until 30 minutes into the second half, when the amateurs began to tire visibly. The Newcastle team had showed right from the start of this half, 'by the jumpiness of their defence and the fury and speed of their attacks, how important they thought that the next goal, either way, was the one that would matter' (*Daily Mail*).

For the Corinthians, now 'limping and dog-tired', that equaliser must have been a severe blow, but worse was to follow when Jenkins was injured and couldn't continue. With no substitutes allowed in those days the ten amateurs could only defend valiantly what was now a hopeless cause. The final score of 3-1 to Newcastle was no disgrace, and the quality and courage of the team's display won them many new friends.

In the evening the Newcastle team and their entourage were the guests of the Corinthians at a dinner in their London hotel. There, perhaps, some of the talk among the players might have been the amazing fact that neither Gallagher, the professional goal-scoring machine, nor Norman, the amateur equivalent, had managed to put his name on the scoresheet. Or perhaps Norman ragged Hughie about his 'missed sitter from no more than ten yards' in the second half! Much later, Norman did reflect that if they had managed a draw they might have had difficulty in putting a team on the field for a replay, as so many of them were carrying injuries from the match or were simply exhausted by their efforts.

Although the crowd at the Newcastle match was the biggest Norman played for in the whole of his career, it was eclipsed significantly by the aggregated attendance at the club's epic encounters with Second Division Millwall in the 1929-30 season. It took the professional side three games in the 3rd round of the cup before they progressed. The crowds were 45,000 at the Crystal Palace, 33,000 at Millwall and 58,000 at Chelsea's Stamford Bridge, giving a total for the tie of 136,000. Norman drily commented to Doggart, who had also played in the three matches, "We didn't win but at least the club's share of the receipts will help to pay the rent on the Crystal Palace ground for a year or two".

Besides his football in Britain, Norman was also very keen on the role of the Corinthians' overseas tours. These tours had been started in 1897 with a visit to South Africa and had continued until the start of the First World War. European countries were the main venues, although Canada, the USA and Brazil were also visited. The principal aim was to spread the Corinthian ideal but also, in some cases, to encourage the game to be played. Little did they know how quickly some of these countries would learn!

Norman's involvement could only start after he had left Cambridge, by which time the tours were primarily to use the sport to mend or foster international relations. The tours took place during the Easter breaks, which allowed schoolmasters such as Norman to take part. The only exception to this was the tour to Canada and the USA in the summer of 1924, although due to his school duties Norman was only available for the month of August and as a result he returned to Dauntsey's at the end of the Canadian fixtures.

The results of the tour games indicate that the strongest Corinthian sides were not always available. Even so, more matches were won than lost, but in any case winning was not the main purpose.

Of the six tours Norman took part in, the one he enjoyed most was the one to Germany and Austria in 1925, when Lilian accompanied him. The team played well in Germany, being unbeaten in their three games. Hamburg, the previous season's German champions, were beaten 4-1 on Easter Sunday, 'largely due to the efforts of Creek, who achieved a hat-trick'. The party were lavishly wined and dined by their hosts; nothing it seemed was too much trouble.

They were also taken on sightseeing tours of Cologne, Hamburg and Berlin. It must have brought back memories to Norman when he saw that the Rhine bridges were being guarded by soldiers of the British Army of Occupation. As they passed through the Ruhr valley, he must have remembered the surveillance flights he had made over the area in 1919. When they crossed into Austria Norman, and indeed all the club members, must have been almost overcome by the effusive welcome in an Austrian paper before the game against the professional side of Vienna: 'Corinthians - For the first time after the Great War we have today the opportunity to welcome a British amateur team within the city of Vienna. A markstone in the history of Austrian sport. YOU, Corinthians of England, who stand foremost for the cry, 'sport for sport's sake'. You come to us, not only as real sportsmen, as true champions of fair play, but also as carriers of a mission of peace, as standard-bearers for the spirit of international sport and the reconciliation of nations through sport.' The cheering of the 50,000 crowd before, during and after the match showed just how heartfelt those sentiments were.

Norman's playing career was a lengthy one but he didn't just fade away. In 1930, when he was thirty-two, he scored a hat-trick against Young Boys of Berne (Swiss Cup winners that year) on the Corinthians' Easter tour. Two months after his thirty fourth birthday, he was selected to play for England in the Amateur International match against Scotland at Hampden Park, Glasgow. Then in his last match for Corinthians (against Wiltshire FA), at the age of thirty eight, he scored four goals. His touch hadn't deserted him.

I have no doubt that Lilian, and the rest of the family, were very proud of Norman's achievements on the football field, but at least his retirement meant that she had one less chore to do. After every match the Corinthian players, or their wives or girlfriends, had to remove the club badges from their football shirts before washing and ironing them and then sew the badges back on ready for the next match. Behind every great man there stands a woman!

A biplane which FNS flew in WW1

Family group: back row FNS; his father; brother Reginald
Front row: Lilian (his fiancée); brother Charles; his mother

Trinity College Football X1: FNS middle row, second from left

Trinity College Athletics team; FNS standing on the right, second back row

HIS DAY.—Creek, the Corinthian forward, crowned a fine display in their match against Clapton Orient by scoring both goals. Here he is netting the second. Corinthians won 2—1.
—(*Daily Sketch.*)

Scoring for Corinthians v Clapton Orient -
the caption from the Daily Sketch says it all!

Another of the 146 goals FNS scored for Corinthians

FNS in 1925

FNS ('the Hairpin') caricatured by Fred May, a major cartoonist of the day

FNS, the schoolmaster. Dauntseys School staff portrait

The 'Teach Yourself' books written by FNS

CHAPTER SIX

THE CRICKETING YEARS

1925-54

War? What war? On August 4th 1914 this could have been the view of some of the members of the MCC, cricket's ruling body. The First World War had started, but the English First Class Cricket Championship was in full swing. However, in the weeks that followed there was mounting concern among the general public and, in a letter to *The Sportsman* dated August 27th, Dr W G Grace, now retired but still very much revered, summed up the mood of the nation: "The time has arrived when the county cricket season should be closed, for it is not fitting at a time like this that able-bodied men should be playing day by day, and pleasure seekers look on... I should like to see all first-class cricketers of suitable age set a good example, and come to the help of their country without delay in its hour of need."

Although there was some alteration to fixtures,

notably when the Oval ground was taken over by the Army, the competition wound on to its September conclusion with Surrey emerging as the champions. Belatedly, cricket fell into line with other sporting events and after the 1914 season there were no more championship matches until the war ended. However, in each of the two years 1917 and 1918, several matches were played in aid of charities raising money for war wounded and their dependents. Then in late August 1919, a representative two-day match between the Army and the RAF was played at Kennington Oval, the home of Surrey County Cricket Club. With the lack of competitive cricket for the previous three years the two teams which took the field might have been considered by some to be 'scratch' teams, but close examination of the credentials of the twenty-two individuals involved would have given the lie to that idea. More than half of them had played first class cricket up to 1914, two of them had captained championship winning counties (Warwickshire 1911; Surrey 1914) and four were to be Test players in the following few years.

Probably the greatest was George Geary, Leicestershire and England, who famously bowled Bradman in the 1934 Nottingham Test. If Norman was over-awed to be in such exalted company it didn't show in his bowling performance. The Army scored 387 in their first innings, but Norman was the best of the RAF bowlers with three wickets for 65 runs (including the wicket of Geary). The RAF fared badly in their first innings, being bowled out for only 99 with Norman failing to trouble the scorer. However, following on, the RAF batted with much greater resolve. Norman was eventually one of George Geary's six victims but not before he had scored 101 out of a total of 357, which virtually ensured that the game was drawn.

In its account of the game, *The Sportsman* of 19th August stated: 'The RAF against a powerful Army eleven accomplished an excellent performance at Kennington Oval... Creek hit fourteen fours in his century knock'. On the evidence of this match, Norman would have been a strong candidate for a place with one of the south western First Class counties (Hampshire, Somerset, or Gloucestershire). According to those who played with him and against him in later years, he was a forcing right-hand batsman, a medium fast bowler and a splendid fielder who would have been an asset to most sides.

In the 1919 season, taking advantage of 'daylight saving time', brought in as a wartime measure to help farm workers, all the First Class county matches were played over two days rather than three as they had been before the war. But this experiment wasn't considered a success, as there were too many drawn games, so the 1920 season saw the three-day format reinstated. Norman must have realised that once he was establishing himself at Dauntsey's, and being involved with Corinthians including their tours, there was no way that he could fit in three-day matches, so First Class cricket was not for him.

His involvement in the 1924 Summer tour to Canada, taking up all of August, meant that even two-day cricket couldn't be contemplated before the 1925 season at the earliest.

Norman had been a keen cricketer even in his grammar school days, so once established at West Lavington, the location of Dauntsey's School, he began to look for opportunities to play. He didn't have to look very far. The Awdrys, one of the major families in the area, owned private grounds near the school and all three of their sons played Minor Counties cricket for Wiltshire. The family also had a reputation for providing good cricket and even better hospitality. At that time the family was very much the driving force behind Wiltshire cricket. Colonel Robert William played for the county before the war, captained it after the war and acted as honorary secretary and treasurer. However, despite Norman's performance against 'The Army' six years previously, and his developing friendship with the Awdrys, he couldn't expect to walk into the county side. He had to show his ability, first having a few games for Devizes, and then in two-day matches for the Wiltshire Club and Ground side against good standard touring sides made up of amateurs with a sprinkling of ex professionals. Matches against Free Foresters, Eton Ramblers, and Old Wykehamists gave him the opportunity to show his worth.

He was mainly used as a bowler at first and didn't disappoint, with figures of 6 for 94, 4 for 48, 3 for 14, 5 for 88 and 2 for 29. Then he was moved up the batting order and struck such good form that he headed the batting averages for the season with an average of 57. As a result of these performances he was selected for the last three county matches of the 1926 season. He would have enjoyed the settings for the games; all fine grounds with typically English surroundings – Salisbury for the home match against Dorset, the Marlborough College ground for the away match against Berkshire and the Blandford Forum ground for the return match with Dorset. He would also have had some satisfaction in playing Minor Counties cricket, but I am sure he would have been most disappointed with his efforts. He didn't shine with the ball - 2 for 64, 0 for 80 and 0 for 86, and didn't bat in three of the six Wiltshire innings. If that had been what the selectors had to remember him for over the winter months he might not have been on their team sheets in 1927. Fortunately, in the game against Berkshire, although coming in to bat at No. 10, he scored an excellent 80.

It was also fortunate that for much of his innings he was watched from the opposite end of the pitch by Charles Awdry, who made a century. That innings may have been the reason why the selectors persevered with him in the 1927 and 1928 seasons, although they still viewed him primarily as a bowler. Producing figures of 6 for 94 against Free Foresters and 2 for 22 and 3 for 77 against Dorset, he justified their faith in him. But he was also, in his lower order batting position, producing useful runs such as 38 not out against Kent 2nd XI, and as a result, he gradually found himself being pushed further up the batting order. By the end of the 1930 season the man heading the batting averages for Wiltshire County was none other than F N S Creek!

In that season he scored what proved to be his highest score for the county – 124 not out against Dorset. He also topped the club and ground averages with 76 and a top score of 100 not out (in that same list Nigel Balchin, the novelist, appears fifth with an average of 31.5).

By the mid 1930s Norman had settled into being a middle-order batsman and only a very occasional bowler. Although he was still remarkably fit, as shown by his footballing exploits, he was more than happy to pass the fast bowling mantle on to younger colleagues. In total he played twenty-one times for the county before the Second World War. Once that conflict had started he, like so many others, was involved with more serious matters. However, in 1942 he took part in a match between a Devizes and District XI and an RAF XI in aid of the British Red Cross. The RAF side contained several players attached to First Class counties including Sgt. Brookes, who five years later was in the Test team facing the West Indies. The Devizes side was also bolstered by three locally-based Army men with County or Lancashire League experience. It was an evening match and a good crowd ensured that £22 was sent to the Red Cross (the equivalent of more than £800 today).

The RAF XI batted first and with Brookes batting well before being bowled by Creek, they declared on 118 for 6. Norman took 2 for 21. Devizes had ninety minutes in which to make the runs. Norman, batting at number three, came to the crease with the score on 17 for 1. Seymour Gann, in his report for the local paper, wrote:

When Boyce was bowled Creek came in and took such toll of his first over from Mook that Barnes immediately brought himself on. Creek's innings was quite the outstanding feat of the evening. He cut and drove superbly, and despite the speed at which he made his runs, made only three false strokes one of which gave a very difficult chance in the slips. However, after opening bat Jeffreson (a Bradford League player) had left, Creek received little support. He was sixth out at 85, a mis-timed drive resulting in a neat catch at extra cover, for 47, in which he hit a six and seven fours.'

Devizes fell short by 13 of the runs required when their innings closed.

After the war ended Norman played again for Wiltshire, although he was now in his late forties. His last match for them, at Chippenham against Kent's 2nd XI on 26th August 1946, must have been a particular source of pride for him, as it was also the debut match for his eighteen-year-old son, Carey. Wiltshire were well beaten, but out of a very low 1st innings score of 66 Norman made 22. Carey struggled, as did most of the other Wiltshire batsmen, but he went on to play well for the county in the 1950s, scoring his maiden century for them against the Kent 2nd XI. Carey also played county hockey for Wiltshire and then Northamptonshire - the Creek sporting gene was alive and well.

Although Norman had retired from the Wiltshire county cricket scene, he couldn't resist when it was suggested that he might like to join a group of enthusiasts who played cricket for (serious!) fun. They had no ground to call their own and the founders of the 'club' in the 1930s couldn't think of a suitable name for their team, so on all correspondence they used a question mark until someone could come up with an idea. No-one did, so they simply took the name 'The Wiltshire Queries'!

Through contacts, they used any pitches which happened to be available in the area and played against any opponents prepared to take them on. Carey, who remembers having many enjoyable games for the Queries with his father, told me that to be a member you had to be 'a good chap', a keen cricketer, have an excess of humour, and be able to contribute to the club with bat or ball. Most of the members were schoolmasters, so all the games were played in the summer holidays. Matches were played at Chippenham, Marlborough, Devizes, and Swindon. Also at Bowerchalke 'where players had to be there well before the scheduled start of play as cows and their deposits had to be moved off before battle could commence'.

Norman continued playing with the Queries until he left Dauntsey's school in 1954 and moved out of the area to take up his role with The Football Association. (The Wiltshire Queries are still in existence today, 2013).

CHAPTER SEVEN

WRITER AND JOURNALIST

1930-63

The Corinthian Football Club was founded in the 1882-83 season, one of its main objects being to improve the performance of the England Amateur team, especially against their arch-rivals Scotland. An early history of the club, 'Annals of the Corinthian FC' by B O Corbett, had been published in 1906, but by 1930 the committee felt an updated version was needed. Many changes had taken place to the club, and to football in general, before and after the First World War, and the coming 50th anniversary of the club seemed to be an appropriate time for a new book.

The problem was finding someone who could take on the mammoth task of dealing with the statistics of fifty years of club matches, including their overseas tours, interview past players for their views and anecdotes, and weave the story of the club into the fabric of an evolving and increasingly professional national game. I suspect Norman's name was put forward by his friend, A G (Graham) Doggart. Norman had serious doubts about having the ability or the time, but the founder of the club, N L 'Pa' Jackson, whose memories of the early days and enthusiasm for the club were second to none, persuaded him otherwise. It was a challenge, and Norman never shirked challenges. However, he was a full-time teacher, not an author, and it took more than two years to complete the necessary research, collate the material, then write an interesting, informative book worthy of the subject.

Fortunately the Doggarts lived in London and Norman was very grateful that Mrs. Doggart "spent much time in monotonous research in the British Museum in order that the statistical and other details in these pages should be as accurate as possible". The book was published by Longmans in 1933, to widespread critical acclaim. Reviews in national newspapers such as *The Observer* and *The Manchester Guardian*, and more provincial ones such as *The Yorkshire Post* and *The Oxford Times* were all in agreement. "This is an excellent book and should be on the shelves in every sportsman's library" said the Sussex Daily News.

Norman was delighted with the response, especially as the following extract from his Author's Preface indicates his unsureness of his credentials as a writer: "This work has been compiled by one who is essentially an amateur writer, whose work, defective as it may be, is possibly leavened by another amateur characteristic – keenness. Chambers defines an amateur as 'one who cultivates a particular study for the love of it'. In the spirit of that definition this book has been produced."

The club committee was equally pleased, as shown by the letter which arrived at the Creek's household, Skelwyth, Dauntsey's School:

My dear Norman, I have been requested by the committee to write a very special letter of thanks to you on behalf of the Corinthian Football Club for the very great service you have rendered in compiling 'A History of the Corinthian Football Club', and for all the hard work you so willingly undertook in preparing it. With the same thoroughness, brilliance and tireless energy which you have always displayed in your many appearances for the Club on the field, you have successfully carried through a very difficult task, which only one man in a thousand would even have undertaken. By your labours, you have created a very full record of all the battles fought by our famous old Club since its inception. May this great work of yours inspire the hearts, heads and feet of countless Corinthians who follow in your footsteps. Yours sincerely, J G Stevenson (Secretary).

The success of the book not only encouraged Norman to consider further forays into print but alerted editors of sporting and general interest magazines and journals to his talent in this field. Consequently the mid 1930s saw many articles appearing under his name in various magazines. Topics included: 'Explanation of the new off-side rule', 'The value of football in international relations', 'Is modern sport a good thing?', 'Tips from the touchline', 'Which sport for Johnnie?', 'Story of the Olympic Games' and many others.

His work also appeared across the Atlantic. The November 1934 issue of the magazine *The Rotarian* contained a five-page article entitled 'Football on its Native Heath'. In the article Norman traced the development of English Association Football (Soccer) and how it differed from rugby football and American football. He also described the skills and tactics involved in playing the game. Photographs and illustrations accompanied the text. However, he must have been a little dismayed and/or amused by the editor allowing drawings of (English) soccer players heading a football wearing baseball caps!

As a result of his writings and his coaching of schoolboys in many sports, as well as an increasing number of lectures to groups of coaches, Norman was beginning to be looked upon as a guru in the sports coaching world. J M Dent and Sons, the publishers, were in the process of producing a series of books on 'Modern Sports' and Norman was asked to write the volume on Association Football. The series editor, Howard Marshall, wrote in the foreword to the book: 'In this important volume, the game is considered in its entirety by a writer who combines an exceptionally wide playing experience with an unusually keen analytical and logical mind. I do not think it is extravagant to claim that Mr Creek has given us what will with justice be recognized for many years to come as the standard textbook on Association Football'.

The book was written for everyone interested in the game – players, administrators, officials, spectators. Even hardened professionals in the game could well learn something from the appendix, where the Rules of the Game are written – this was particularly relevant as in the year the book appeared Mr C E Sutcliffe, President of The Football League, was bemoaning the fact that he thought "less than ten per cent of the players in football today know the minor points of the game".

Reviews in the sporting press were unanimous in their praise. The following extract from the Yorkshire Post is typical: "A copy of this book should be put in every clubroom, at least two copies in every school library, and the man in the crowd who reads it will almost certainly be the better equipped both to appreciate and to criticise the games he goes to see".

After the start of the Second World War Norman's time outside teaching was taken up with his liaison work between the ATC and the RAF. Any thoughts of writing had to be put aside. Once the war had been won and life began to return to something approaching normality, he assumed his writing days were over, even though Dent brought out a reprint of his book in 1947. However, another publisher, The English Universities Press Ltd, had their eye on the leisure interests and sports coaching market. In what proved to be a major coup in the post-war book world they brought out a series of 'Teach

Yourself' books, edited by Leonard Cutts, which were an immediate commercial success. Norman became much involved and wrote six books: *Teach Yourself Soccer*, published in 1949, *Teach Yourself Cricket* (1950) *Teach Yourself Rugby Football* (1950), *Teach Yourself Hockey* (1951), *Teach Yourself Lawn Tennis* (1952) and *Teach Yourself Athletics* (1954). There was also a junior Teach Yourself book, *Soccer for Boys*, published in 1951. These books proved so popular that Doggart was moved to ask Norman if he didn't think it unusual that the two most widely-read current authors writing in English were both called Norman. "And of the two it wouldn't surprise me if Mailer was in second place", he added. At that time Norman Mailer was one of the rising stars on the American literary scene.

"Writing factual books and coaching manuals only takes time and effort", Norman replied. "I wish I did have the talent to write fiction but you can only work with what you are given."

The last of his coaching manuals was written and published while he was still a schoolmaster. However, in that year (1954) he moved from Dauntsey's School to the Football Association as Assistant Director of Coaching (a later chapter will deal with that phase of his life). His new role meant there was little or no time for writing other than the occasional article in annuals such as the FA Book for Boys. However, 1963 was the centenary of the Association and Norman felt moved to mark the occasion in verse:

The Centenary of The Football Association

One Hundred Years! A century of Time
Has winged its way across the football seasons;
And you and I, who played it in our prime,
For friendship, fun, and other sporting reasons,
All owe a debt of gratitude to those –
In counsel far surpassing their vocation –
Who just one hundred years ago this month
United all in one Association.
'Twas ever thus. From humblest of beginnings
When pioneers have started on their way,
Our founders' thoughts were local in their outlook –
They only wanted rules that all might play.
And yet their legislation had great vision,
Though laws and plans were mainly for the few
The tender plant became a mighty forest
As soccer football grew and grew – and grew.
From Schools and Old Boys, Lancashire and Sheffield,
From Oxford and from Cambridge, and from Stoke,
From Nottingham and Bristol, Leeds and London –
This game just suited every kind of folk –
Its priceless asset is that it is class-less,
But, as we turn the pages of the book,
We note with pride our status has developed
To Royal Patron, Presidential Duke.
All praise to you again, then, FA Founders,
Whose foresight means so much to us today,
Your game whose hundredth birthday we would honour

More than a hundred nations now can play.
As country after country swells the numbers,
With each new football flag that is unfurled
The message comes from every game and pastime,
That "soccer is the greatest in the world".

This may not be Laureate standard but well deserves a place in any anthology of Poetry and Sport!

CHAPTER EIGHT

BEHIND THE MICROPHONE

1936-54

Norman's next venture was into broadcasting. The 1936
FA Cup Final between Arsenal and Sheffield United
which could be considered the real beginning of his long
association with the microphone came about by chance.
The previous year, the co-commentators had been Ivan
Sharpe, a journalist, and George Allison, the manager
of Arsenal. Mr Allison, who had much experience of
broadcasting, asked the BBC to release him from his
contract, as he felt 'his first duty must be to support the
Arsenal players'.

No immediate replacement was available, but
discussions between the BBC and Stanley Rous, the
recently appointed FA secretary, came up with the
name of a substitute – F N S Creek. Norman had only
the slightest experience of the role (in 1934 he had
taken over the broadcast of the second half of the

England v. Germany match when the commentator fell ill), but he approached it in his typically thorough way. In the photo shoots of the two teams in the days before the game he was there to familiarise himself with the players to enable him to quickly recognize them on the field of play. As a result of this and his natural microphone manner the broadcast was a great success. Letters to the Programme Director at the BBC, expressing their delight at Norman's work, were received from listeners as far afield as Otago, New Zealand and New Brunswick, Canada. The Daily Express of 7th December 1936 added its voice to the chorus of approval with, "Keep Mr Creek on as a permanent commentator – he's the fastest, snappiest, most human, and entertaining we've had in a long time. And he really knows his football".

From that moment on Norman's broadcasting career took off, almost mirroring the meteoric rise he had enjoyed in his playing days. As the first television coverage of football did not start until the Cup Final of 1938 and very few households had TV sets (at the end of 1947 there were only 54,000 licensed receivers), it was the Outside Broadcasting Department of BBC Radio the sporting public relied upon if they were unable to attend the events themselves. Commentators were in demand; good ones particularly so.

The next football season, 1936-37, saw a gradual increase in the number of live radio broadcasts. There was also an improvement in microphones, making the job of the commentator a little easier. However, the commentator's box varied greatly from ground to ground – those at Wembley stadium and at Arsenal's Highbury ground were well positioned centrally in the main stand and had all the facilities needed, but many others were literally boxes on top of a stand with rudimentary cover from the elements and were reached by means of scaffolding ladders. At these grounds the commentators not only needed a good microphone voice but had to be nimble and have a good head for heights. Fortunately Norman had.

In these pre-Second World War days of outside broadcasts the commentators of major national events were given VIP treatment. Norman experienced this when he was brought in as the commentator for the 1939 Amateur Cup Final at Roker Park, Sunderland between two County Durham teams, Willington and Bishop Auckland. He was allowed first-class travel from London King's Cross to Newcastle on the LNER's 'Silver Jubilee', Britain's first Streamline train. Car transport was provided from West Lavington to London and from Newcastle to Sunderland, and on the train journey home there was a very good choice for dinner!

However, Norman was a full-time schoolteacher, so he could usually only provide commentaries for matches within easy travelling distance of his home. Bournemouth, Swindon and Bristol matches were covered for the West of England region, with the occasional talk on sport-related matters recorded at the

Bristol studio for a mid-week transmission. This opportunity to record programmes in advance, at times which did not conflict with his teaching commitments, opened another chapter in his radio work. *Children's Hour* provided Norman with an excellent opportunity to reach a wider audience with his views on sport in general and his 'Tips from the Touchline'. *Children's Hour* had started in 1922 and had built up a good reputation, with a varied programme of topics aimed at the under fifteens. In 1938 Norman was 40 and had two children in the target age group. He was also a schoolteacher, and I rather think he would have felt a certain affinity with the source of the programme's title, taken from a verse of Longfellow: 'Between the dark and the daylight/When the night is beginning to lower/Comes a pause in the day's occupations/That is known as the Children's Hour.'

He first broadcast for the BBC on the 6th September 1938 on The National Home Service, and by the 12th September 1950 he had made one hundred broadcasts. A special compilation was made by the BBC to mark the occasion. As well as coaching tips on the popular sports he interviewed many of the outstanding sportspersons of the day for the children's programmes. These included Frank Swift, the Manchester City and England goalkeeper; Denis Compton, the Middlesex and England batsman; Harold Abrahams, Olympic athlete; Eddie Hapgood, the Arsenal and England fullback; Learie Constantine, West Indian cricketer;

Alison Cridland, international netball player; and Dan Maskell, the tennis coach and later BBC commentator.

Just how important the youngsters of the day considered these broadcasts to be was related to me by 86-year-old George Almond of Sunderland:

"My brother and I used to run home from junior school on the days he was broadcasting, to get all the jobs done our mother had lined up for us, to make sure we didn't miss the programme. Then the next day at school we'd talk about it to our friends who had also listened to it. F N S was an important part of our sports education".

Although he was still doing live outside broadcasts of football matches in 1938 and 1939, the outbreak of war on 3rd September 1939 caused a major change in the organisation of football in England. Three matches had been played by all the league teams by 2nd September, but the government stopped further matches taking place by bringing in emergency measures. The first of these was to ban the assembly of crowds, although this was quickly changed to allow attendances of 8,000, and by 14th September revised to 15,000. But in these early, frantic wartime weeks few aspects of life could remain untouched. Many professional footballers had already joined the Armed Forces, and a further Government ruling bringing in a 50-mile limit for all non-essential travel meant league football could not resume in its previous format.

However, on more considered reflection of the

situation, the Government inclined to the view that some form of football would be good for the morale of the nation. Consequently the Football League placed all the league clubs into seven regional areas in which all the clubs were within the 50-mile travelling limit. Problems still arose, as the local police and the Home Office had to give their permission for every match, and sometimes fear of a bombing raid caused last-minute refusal.

From the fans' point of view there was an up side to these ad hoc arrangements, as players who had joined one of the various services were allowed to make 'guest' appearances for clubs near where they were stationed. Aldershot fans were particularly fortunate, as Army and RAF bases in the town resulted in more than twenty internationals 'guesting' for the club during the war years. Other clubs were less fortunate – Swindon, where Norman made several match commentaries in 1939 and even one in February 1940, had their ground requisitioned as a prisoner of war camp, as did Preston North End.

Further to all this, and with special dispensation, a new knock-out competition was started – The Football League War Cup. The first final was played in 1940 and West Ham United beat Blackburn Rovers 1-0. Norman wasn't involved, as his work for *Children's Hour* and on programmes for the Forces at home and overseas was beginning to take up more of his time. However, the following year he was a co-commentator at Wembley stadium, where Preston North End played a 1-1 draw against Arsenal, and the following week at Blackburn Rovers Ground where Preston won the replay 2-1.

Norman, because of his experience in this particular role, was probably considered to be the senior man behind the microphone, but the man sharing the commentating duties with him was very much a star in his own right. Stanley Holloway was well known for his radio, theatre and film work. At this particular time he had made some morale boosting propaganda films for Pathé News and the BBC, and his broadcasting of a football match when the Luftwaffe were still making nightly bombing raids across London was probably thought to be a further indication that Britain was not to be cowed.

In that same year (1941) the ATC was formed, and as indicated earlier, Norman was very much involved. It also resulted in him contributing to many programmes targeted at those in uniform. Some were aimed at particular areas such as 'Forces in the East' and 'The Middle East and North Africa', while others were more generally broadcast 'for men and women abroad'. However, the BBC did not ignore the servicemen and women serving in Britain, and at 5.15 pm Monday and Thursday, 'Ack-Ack, Beer-Beer' was broadcast on the Home Service for 'Anti-Aircraft, Searchlight and Balloon Barrage units'. This was a magazine-style programme to which many personalities of the day contributed, including Lionel Gamlin, Peter West and Tommy Trinder. Norman discussed current sporting issues. The aim was to bring a sense of normality into the listeners' lives.

Norman also worked with Tommy Trinder on a series of six programmes for the Forces entitled *Kings of Sport*. The two men proved to be a very good choice of compères, as they shared wide sporting interests including a passion for football (Trinder, as well as being a very popular comedian, was Chairman of Fulham Football Club).

Children's Hour broadcasts were continuing to feature large in Norman's life, made possible by their being pre-recorded. His talks on a great variety of sports must have been a popular feature as he continued with them, with some sports quiz items, into the 1950s. However, one item ruffled some feathers. In 1944 Norman gave a broadcast on the work of the ATC and the importance of the organisation. Some listeners took exception to this, as they felt 16 and 17-year-olds could feel demeaned by the topic being on a children's programme. The BBC printed its reasons in the *Radio Times* of August 25th 1944. They were obviously happy with the item and its *Children's Hour* slot, as on 30th April 1946 Norman did an extended talk on gliding and the ATC and its usefulness for would-be pilots.

With the end of the war in 1945, although the regional leagues were continued for one more season, football commentaries returned to their pre-war national coverage and Norman was quite heavily involved, covering 12 matches, including the FA Cup semi-final between Charlton Athletic and Bolton Wanderers and the Amateur Cup Final between Barnet and Bishop Auckland.

That summer he also made his début as a cricket commentator, for the match at Taunton between Somerset and Gloucestershire. But things were changing in the world of sports broadcasting. The BBC began to engage more full-time commentators for major events. Raymond Glendenning had been full-time since 1932, joining as a graduate entrant, but by 1942 he was Assistant Director of Outside Sports Broadcasts and by 1946 he had become the leading sports commentator. Rex Alston, like Norman, was a schoolmaster and part-time commentator, but he left his position at Bedford School and joined the staff of the BBC, eventually specialising in First Class and Test Match cricket. Others, such as John Arlott and Peter West, were added to the growing band of full-time broadcasters.

Norman, who by now had worked with Glendenning on many occasions, must have been asked to join the group. But such a role wasn't for him. Reporting on sport was one thing, but it didn't have the teaching, coaching aspect which really drove him. The BBC were still keen to use him and probably hoped they might be able to persuade him to change his mind. In the 1946-47 football season he was the commentator at several important league games including Tottenham Hotspur v Newcastle United, Aston Villa v Middlesbrough and Chelsea v Everton. Then, to round off the season he had the plum jobs of the England v Wales Amateur international at Dulwich Hamlet, the Amateur Cup Final (Wimbledon v Leytonstone) at Arsenal's Highbury stadium and, on the 26th April 1947, most prestigious of all, the FA Cup Final at Wembley stadium between Burnley and Charlton Athletic. This was to be the pinnacle of his football commentary work.

By the start of the next season he was being used more and more as a summariser to the commentaries of Glendenning, although, perhaps significantly in the light of his future role away from teaching, he was still the main commentator for the Amateur Cup Final. But all thoughts on such matters were very much pushed to one side in August 1948. The XIV Modern Olympiad (Olympic Games) was to be held in London, and the BBC brought together a team of twenty-six commentators to cover the seventeen sports. Norman was involved in two: the football tournament, along with Raymond Glendenning and the hockey tournament, with Peter West. As well as commentaries and summaries, talks on the prospects of the different teams had to be given.

In eleven days from 3rd August, Norman made seventeen broadcasts, including the commentary on the football final at Wembley in which Sweden beat Yugoslavia 3-1. This Olympic Games was called the 'Austerity' Olympics, as many countries taking part, especially the European ones, found it difficult to finance their teams as well as they would have wished, and Britain was unable to provide the facilities or the opening and closing ceremonies which are today considered the norm.

A further indication of how times have changed is illustrated in the list of 'General Suggestions' given by the BBC to each of their commentators. Among the points mentioned were these:

- Avoid incorrect use of "English", "Colonial", etc. It is Great Britain that has entered a team not England.

- Avoid "foreigner" and "foreign" if another word will serve.

- "Coloured" is an acceptable way of describing an American negro.

- Refer to a "Chinese" and not a "Chinaman".

- Be careful about showing partisanship. When a British athlete does badly, "That's bad luck for Britain" is unexceptionable, but simply "That's bad luck" makes the commentator seem to take sides.

- Make no excuses for Britain's failures and avoid controversies.

All this is a far cry from today's ubiquitous medals table list and the focus on Britain's stars.

After the Olympics, Norman's radio work became much more focused on sport in the western region and for six months he introduced the weekly programme *Sport in the West Country* for the West of England Home Service. His football commentary work was mainly with matches played by Portsmouth, Southampton, Swindon and the two Bristol clubs, although in January 1949 he was at Yeovil to see them play Sunderland in an FA Cup 4th round match. The result of this game reverberated through the English football world. Sunderland of the First Division was known as the 'Bank of England club', as it had spent so much money buying players. Yeovil was a non-league club which, according to all the pundits, had no chance of coming out on top. "What do they know?" said the fans, and they were right! Yeovil, on their small ground with a sloping pitch, a packed, partisan crowd, a player-manager, Alec Stock, who refused to countenance defeat and eleven players who played the game of their lives, came out on top 2-1 after extra time. As Norman wrote in a newspaper article, 'In the most dramatic Cup upset Yeovil outmanoeuvred, out-paced and outclassed Sunderland in every department'.

But Yeovil had had their moment. In the next round, away to Manchester United, a game which Norman summarised to Raymond Glendenning's commentary, they lost 8-0. At least their share of the gate receipts from a crowd of 80,000 would have tempered their disappointment on the journey back to Somerset.

Norman continued with his *Children's Hour* talks, and also took part in an increasing number of quiz programmes, acting as quizmaster for boys and girls from various schools and organisations in the West Country. In one of them, teams of mothers and daughters took part, and they included his wife Lilian and their daughter Heather.

Another, very different, type of series was with Dr. Ludwig Koch, well known for his recordings of birdsong. In six recorded programmes Norman and Dr. Koch discussed the calls of birds which live in very different habitats in Britain. This series proved so popular that a further six programmes were transmitted.

In these post-war years there was one particular annual radio event that came to be the preserve of two men, The FA Amateur Cup Final, with Raymond Glendenning listed as the commentator and 'expert' summaries to be given by F N S Creek. They covered every final from 1946 to 1953. The 1951 match between Bishop Auckland and Pegasus was particularly memorable, thanks to an injury suffered by Jimmy Nimmins, the Bishop Auckland midfielder. He was renowned for his ferocious but fair tackling, but it was only after the match was finished that he was found to have played for much of the second half with a cracked tibia. The wide reporting of this added fuel to the generally-held view that the Northern (amateur) League was the toughest in the country at that time.

Another series of football coaching broadcasts, twenty-two in all from May to September 1952, was directed at Indonesia, at the request of their national association. It was titled *It's A Goal*. Norman was particularly happy with this series, as it not only allowed him to 'wear his coaching hat' but fitted in with his view of football being the worldwide sport.

Although the bulk of Norman's broadcasting - over 500 broadcasts in total - was in radio, he did make some appearances in front of the television cameras. The first, in the early days of TV, was in July 1939. It was a discussion programme chaired by A G Street with a group of people who were well known in sport. These included Harold Abrahams (athletics), George Allison (football manager), Henry Longhurst (golf), Bill Tilden (tennis) and W W Wakefield (cricket), as well as Norman. The topic discussed was 'Is Modern Sport a Good Thing?' It would be interesting to know the views expressed, but regrettably no record of their discussion survives.

Norman's next TV appearance was on July 1st 1946 (transmitted on August 26th). This too was a discussion programme chaired by Arthur Street. On this occasion Norman was part of a smaller gathering which included Dan Maskell, Peter Wilson (at that time the foremost sports journalist) and Sir Pelham Warner. Warner was considered to be the foremost authority on cricket. As a player he had captained the MCC on their tours against Australia and South Africa. He had also played both with and against W G Grace, and since retiring from playing, he had been editor of *The Cricketer* magazine. Strangely this programme was actually filmed at the home of the chairman and could have been classed as an Outside Broadcast. The BBC arranged a private coach service from Broadcasting House at the Alexandra Palace to pick up the panellists at pre-arranged points and take them, with the film crew, to and from A G Street's West Country farm. Norman was able to make his own way there from his home in West Lavington. The topic – 'Britain's position in the world of sport at the end of the first year of peace' - was particularly relevant, as very shortly after that the International Olympic Committee invited Britain to stage the Olympic Games of 1948, in which Norman was to cover the football and hockey competitions on radio. However, although he did make the occasional appearance on *The World of Sport*, usually reviewing some forthcoming football match, and was involved in general sporting discussions with up and coming TV presenters such as Eamonn Andrews, Harry Carpenter and Cliff Michelmore, the time involvement required was too great for someone who had a demanding full-time job away from broadcasting. While some might have thought he could put a quart into a pint pot, two quarts was an impossibility.

CHAPTER NINE

ENGLAND'S AMATEUR FOOTBALL SUPREMO

1954-64

After the end of the Second World War there was a great desire among the general population to get back to normality, and in particular to enjoy themselves. As a result, attendances at all manner of leisure activities in Britain soared. The Football League matches for each season from 1946 to 1950 attracted between 35 and 40 million spectators.

Unfortunately those years of 'victory euphoria', wonderful though they seemed at the time, were masking the fact that the post-war world could never be the same as in pre-war days. Football was no exception to this. The England team in 1948 beat Portugal 10-0 and Italy 4 -0 and were one of the favourites to win the 1950 World Cup in Brazil, but it didn't turn out that way. First of all too little attention had been paid to the fact that many European countries, such as Italy, were still recovering from the effects of having been occupied during the war, so our successes against them didn't give a true assessment of our footballing strength. Then in the 1952 Olympic Football tournament in Helsinki, Finland, the English game received a big 'wake-up call'. The Great Britain team, which mainly consisted of English players (all of them amateurs, as the Olympic rules required them to be) failed to reach the first round, losing their preliminary round match to Luxembourg 5-3. That result was disappointing, but it was made more galling by the fact that the competition was won by Hungary, many of whose star players were state funded, as they were officially classed as serving soldiers.

However, amateur or professional, the overall quality of the Hungarians' play impressed everyone including Stanley Rous, the secretary of the FA, who was one of the guests at the final, and he invited them to come to Wembley the following year to take on the full England professional team. The Hungarians not only won that game 6-3 (the first time England had lost a game on home soil), but even more convincingly, they beat England 7-1 in Budapest in 1954. They gave such a magnificent display of skill that it brought home to the authorities the need for proper organised coaching of young players.

Walter Winterbottom had been appointed Director of Coaching in 1946, but his remit was far too wide; at first he was even expected to see to the travel and accommodation arrangements of the national team. By 1953 the Football Association committee was seeking an Assistant Director of Coaching who would be given full responsibility for the development of a coaching organisation for all amateur football in the country and also be the manager/coach of the England amateur team. This would allow Winterbottom to concentrate on the professional game, although his assistant would also be involved in technical and training schemes for all the FA sides.

The search for the right man was quickly over. No one was more eligible for the job than Norman Creek, and so, in 1954, he ended his teaching career at Dauntsey's School to take up this full-time role with the FA. Newspaper comments on his appointment were very favourable. He was well respected as a coach and communicator and was also known as a man with boundless energy and enthusiasm for the game (played in the right manner). Further to this, he had a sound grasp of the evolving tactics in the modern game.

From the FA's point of view it was a good appointment. For Norman it seemed the ideal job, although, as we shall see later, if he had known the effect increasingly large sums of money coming into the game would have on the sport he would almost certainly have had second thoughts. But it seemed a good time to make the move. Although he and Lilian would have to vacate the rented school house, which must have been a wrench for them as it had been the 'family home' for thirty one years, their two children were now adults and making their own way, so the move was acceptable to all.

As he would be based in the FA headquarters at Lancaster Gate, London, he and Lilian would have to live within reasonable travelling distance of the capital. By a stroke of good fortune a house in the village of Syke Cluan, near Iver in Buckinghamshire, came on the market. The FA bought it and rented it to Norman for ten years.

The task of putting in place a structured coaching scheme to cover the whole country and to have the necessary number of qualified coaches to run it was formidable. The way forward, as Norman saw it, was to begin in the teacher training colleges, particularly those specialising in sports. At that time Carnegie College, Leeds, Cardiff and Loughborough were foremost in the field, and it was to them Norman first turned his attention. He was able to draw on the services of a number of coaches who had already gained their FA coaching badges on courses organised by Winterbottom and on which Norman had been one of the head coaches, although on a part-time basis. Some of these were ex-professional players such as Jimmy Frew, formerly of Portsmouth FC, who was Chief Coach to the West Riding FA.

As well as improving the quality of coaching given to students on the sports studies courses, during the summer vacations two-week residential courses were run for schoolmasters and youth leaders. These courses led to the Preliminary Coaching Certificate and, for those who had already achieved that, to the Full Coaching Certificate. A number of what might be termed more enlightened amateur clubs also sent some of their players on these courses. However, new ideas are sometimes resisted and there were reported instances of enthusiastic young coaches armed with their Preliminary badge who were seeking to gain wider experience coaching young players but were 'shown the door' by clubs who saw no reason to change their ways.

Norman was well aware that it would take time, even after the full structure was in place, and fortunately the FA committee also realised this. But time was pressing on his heels, as within a year of his appointment he had to turn his attention to the Olympic Games of 1956, which were to be held in Melbourne, Australia. He had been selected as manager and chief coach of the Great Britain amateur football team. In this role he was following Matt Busby, the manager of Manchester United, who did the job on a part-time basis in London in 1948, and Walter Winterbottom in Helsinki in 1952. In neither of those tournaments had our teams done as well as hoped, so Norman was aware that among the general public there was a level of expectation that there would be an improved performance from the team, and his stock would rise or fall as a result. However, he was equally aware that the odds were stacked against him and his team.

As in 1948 and 1952, the manager was not involved

in the selection of the squad. There was another problem - although the team would play under the Great Britain banner, the football associations of Scotland, Wales, and Northern Ireland decided not to be involved because of the cost of travel to Australia, so the squad would consist only of English players. The English FA committee therefore chose the players. The players would have to take time off work, and not all employers were prepared to give paid leave of absence, so this had to be confirmed with each individual under consideration.

Norman thus received the names of his squad in instalments, just weeks before they were to play preliminary round matches against Bulgaria. This was hardly good preparation for what would be a difficult home and away fixture against an Eastern Bloc country the bulk of whose players were largely state supported.

The GB (English) team played well, but were beaten 2-0 in Sofia and drew 3-3 in the return match at Wembley Stadium. Their Olympic involvement should have ended almost before it had begun. But the long trip to Melbourne was too expensive for many national football associations, and that, together with the political tensions in Europe (the Soviet Union had invaded Hungary earlier that year), caused many withdrawals. The Great Britain team was allowed back into the competition.

Even with this bending of the rules, there were only eleven teams when the tournament started in

November 1956. In the six weeks before they set off for Melbourne, several games were hastily arranged for the squad against a variety of teams, some of them young professionals of League clubs including Arsenal and Newcastle United, and combined sides from the main amateur leagues. The results were somewhat mixed, but Norman was not unduly worried. He was looking for a general improvement in the fitness of the players, and in this he relied heavily on the England trainer, Jack Jennings of Northampton Town FC.

By watching each individual player carefully Norman sought to make improvements in their game. As Derek Lewin, a member of the squad, recalls: "He did this in a quiet, friendly manner. He supported us in every way he could to improve our football and our results, without ever throwing teacups".

The squad and officials left by air on 16th November for the three-day journey (via Karachi, Calcutta, Bangkok, Perth and Sydney) to Melbourne. From the first full day there, Norman ensured the squad was worked hard. They started with a ninety-minute training session which he led at Scotch College, and then for the next ten days they had three training sessions a day, overseen by Norman and Jack Jennings. However, the fates seemed to be conspiring against them, as in a friendly match against the local Moreland team, Dexter Adams, a fullback, tore a cartilage and had to be flown home. Then Mike Pinner, the first choice goalkeeper, split a finger in training and was unavailable for any of their games.

However, on the 26th November when they played Thailand in a first-round match they produced a most heartening result, winning 9-0. Unfortunately it was at a cost, as Bob Hardisty, the captain, suffered a groin strain and the squad was now reduced to thirteen players. Because of the small number of teams in the competition, this win put them into the quarter-finals.

Unfortunately they had only three days to bask in the glory of their win. On the 30th they once again found themselves lining up against the state-sponsored Bulgarians. Despite the frenzied exhortations of British sailors from HMS *Newcastle*, which was anchored in the port - at one point they leapt over the fence to encourage the team - they lost 6-1. However, when the final results were analysed Norman and his players could take some consolation from the fact that only 'non-amateur' teams had taken the medals and that the winner (the Soviet Union) had beaten Bulgaria (GB's conquerors) 2-1 only after extra time in their semi-final match.

Norman, probably more than anyone, must have been saddened at this further indication of the demise of the amateur Olympian which had started in the 1952 Games, and with the way international politics had infiltrated the Games. His Corinthian view of the role of sport in a civilised world was to remain strong all his life. Unfortunately the sporting world, despite his efforts, was slowly but surely changing around him.

Reviewing the tournament, Bernard Joy wrote: "We cannot hold our own with nations who are prepared to evade the definition of amateur in order to parade their best performers. Either we follow suit or we must educate some of our rivals to respect the Olympic oath". Norman could not have said that publicly – it would have been construed as sour grapes - but he would have been very sympathetic to Joy's view.

Once the Games were over, financial considerations could not be completely ignored. To give further justification for the cost of sending the squad, the FA arranged for the return trip to be made by way of Singapore, Malaya and Burma to 'show the flag' there. Three games were played, in Singapore, Kuala Lumpur, and Rangoon, all of them against amateur sides. The team won all three, and the gate receipts brought in a very welcome £1400 for the English FA.

Back in England, Norman continued with his coaching courses, his management of the national amateur team and more broadcasting. As his responsibility was for the development of all amateur football in the country he was concerned about encouraging the game at schoolboy level, and some of his broadcasts were aimed in that direction. To this end there was a talk on radio about the Schoolboys' Course which had been started at the Lilleshall Centre, and for TV, an introduction and coaching analysis of an England v Scotland schoolboys international match at Wembley. However, like Winterbottom in the early 50s, Norman was finding that a lack of staff on the administrative side was hampering his efforts. Embarking on overseas tours with the amateurs was a welcome relief . "They had to get on without me then!" he said.

In May 1957 a mini tour into Europe saw them pitted against 'France Amateurs' at Mulhouse, where they lost 3-1. There was a 1-1 draw against Germany at Offenburg and an excellent 3-2 win at Chaux de Fonds against a Swiss 'B' team. The Swiss were young professionals, so the game doesn't appear in the list of amateur internationals played by England, but it was certainly a good result for them.

In later years Norman, and more recently a grandson, could bring to mind that game because of the Swiss (Venus make) wristwatch which was presented to him as manager of the England team. On the back it is inscribed '16th May 1957 Suisse v Angleterre Amateurs'.

An interesting memory of that tour was related to me by Derek Lewin. Norman and the team flew out from London on an FA-chartered Viscount aircraft which was not pressurised, so it had to fly below a height of 12,000 feet. This meant flying through the Alps rather than over them! From his window seat, Norman called out the names of the towns they were flying over. When asked how he knew, he said he had flown over the area many times when in the Royal Flying Corps in the First World War. This was the first any in the party knew of his involvement in that conflict. It was typical of him – a private, modest man. Indeed it was only years after his death that these players learned of Norman's achievements on the football field.

Amateur international matches against teams representing Scotland, Northern Ireland and Wales were regular features on Norman's calendar in each of his ten years with the FA, but Olympic tournaments and tours were particularly interesting. In 1958 the English FA arranged a tour of West Africa. Of the seventeen players in the party, ten were full-time professionals attached to English League clubs and the rest were amateur internationals. Norman was the manager/coach and he must have been very much in agreement with the prime object of the trip, which was to encourage the development of the game in that area of the world. Seven games were played between 14th May and 3rd June, six of them in various regions of Nigeria (at Lagos, Ibadan, Enugu, Kumasi and Kano). The English team won them all, except the game at Kano which had to be abandoned at half-time due to heavy rain and a violent wind. The other game was in Accra against a Ghanaian team, the first game the Ghanaian team had played under their new name as the country, formerly The Gold Coast, had just gained independence earlier that year. The tour was considered, by both hosts and visitors, to have been a great success.

The next major tour Norman embarked upon as Team Manager was in June 1960, to the West Indies with The Middlesex Wanderers. This was a team of amateur players from England, Scotland and Wales. The Wanderers' touring object was always to spread knowledge of the game, together with an appreciation of how it could help promote sportsmanship and friendship – very much in line with Norman's Corinthian ideals. However, for the seventeen players involved, with the Rome Olympics less than three months away, it was a final chance to impress Norman.

In the space of three weeks they played eight games in six locations in Trinidad, San Fernando, Surinam, Martinique and Jamaica. Despite this heavy schedule for the players they won six of the games, and when the squad for Rome was announced seven of the touring party were included.

1960 was a particularly important year for Norman and for British amateur football. It would turn out to be the last time Great Britain played Olympic football until the 2012 Games in London, and by then the players would all be professionals (all under 23 years of age, but with three over-age players allowed). The 1960 squad of players was again chosen by the FA committee, although Norman did have an input into their deliberations. This time, unlike 1956, the squad was genuinely British, with two players from Northern Ireland, four from Scotland and thirteen from England. There was one unexpected absentee from the English contingent, but on the West Indies tour Norman had taken exception to some ferocious tackling and had bluntly told the player, "We can't take players like you to the Olympics". Norman, the quiet gentleman, was quite capable of taking a stand!

On the wretched business of 'shamateurism' (to be

mentioned in more detail later), where rumours were rife but hard facts were not available until several years afterwards, the make-up of the Rome squad seemed to suggest that the committee and Norman were not unaware of the issue. All the teams entered for the Olympics had to qualify for the finals in Italy by playing preliminary matches, and on the basis of those results the tournament committee placed the competing teams into their first-round groups of four. Norman successfully steered the GB team through these preliminaries. They defeated The Republic of Ireland 3-2 at Brighton & Hove Albion's ground and 3-1 in Dublin, and beat Holland 5-1 in Zwolle and drew 2-2 at Tottenham Hotspur's ground. Consequently they found themselves in one of the strongest groups, with Italy, Brazil and Formosa. That was unfortunate, but it was made worse when in their first game against Brazil in Livorno, they were leading 2-1 when early in the second half Tommy Thompson, one of their fullbacks, suffered a broken leg. With no substitutes allowed they had to complete the game with ten men and they lost 4-3.

Three days later in the Rome Olympic stadium, in front of 45,000 spectators, most of them supporting the home side, they took on Italy. The extracts from a newspaper report pay tribute to their performance:

Through sheer gallant combativity Britain's amateurs drew 2-2 with an Italian XI made up entirely of gifted young professionals, and this before the fanatically partisan Roman crowd... Inspired by the leonine L Brown at centre half they refused to be dismayed, even by the disaster of an early off-side goal and several unpleasant injuries…

Much credit must go to Norman Creek, the manager of the team, whose five sessions at Uxbridge produced such rich rewards both in stamina and teamwork…

The Roman crowd, which had begun characteristically with its deep baying of "EE-TAL-YA!" "EE-TAL-YA!", finished equally characteristically with a scornful chorus of "BU-FFO-NI!" (Clowns) as its own team left the field.

Three days later at Grosseto the British team played Formosa and won 3-2. But three points from their three games weren't enough for them to progress. The newspaper comment - "There is little doubt that were it not for Thompson's injury against Brazil, the courageous British team would have reached the semi-finals" - was probably scant consolation to the party when they flew back from Rome to London the next day, although the British press were of the unanimous opinion that Norman and his team had been extremely unlucky and had done Britain proud.

But problems lay ahead in amateur football in England. During the 1960s there were growing rumours that some amateur clubs were making undercover payments to some of their players, and the practice was growing. The term 'shamateurism' was increasingly mentioned in footballing circles. The FA authorities, including Norman, were not unaware of the situation but could not act on rumours alone.

When Norman retired from the FA in 1963 he was

interviewed by the sports writer Ian Wooldridge, who suggested the FA "had virtually condoned it by apparently pretending that it didn't exist". Norman was not happy. "That's not true. Under-counter payments have been offered to amateurs throughout the whole of my football career. In my last year at Cambridge I was offered an exorbitant sum to play in a First Division side as an amateur. The FA have set up an enquiry. But it's a question of getting the proof. There's a lot of difference between knowing something and getting witnesses to testify to it. The only complete answer would be a proclamation by all amateur clubs. On a given day they would all have to say 'From now on it's to be expenses only'. But so long as clubs are making money from spectators the danger is there".

As it turned out, not only was that danger there but it grew, and eventually, in 1974, the term 'amateur' was ended and with it the FA Amateur Cup and the England Amateur International team. Norman must have been saddened by this – "Lucre had overcome love of the game". But as he said much later (November 1973) in an interview with John Morgan, sportswriter of the Daily Express, "Many factors conspired against the amateur game, but the abolition of the maximum wage for professional footballers made it a nonsense for any talented player who could play in the top grade to remain an amateur".

Although it was not stated in so many words, amateur teams looking to keep their best players would be tempted to give them more than generous expenses if their funds allowed. While there was nothing Norman could have done to prevent the spread of shamateurism, he felt he could use his position to effect a change on another increasing problem in the amateur game – 'rough or dirty play in club matches'. Speaking at a press conference in 1962, he issued a warning that he would refuse to recommend guilty players for international honours. "England players must be above all this. We cannot interfere with club affairs, but I will not stand for it. Although this is a personal warning, I am sure the England committee will back me up. We are now planning for the next Olympics. I'd rather have a squad of decent chaps than any who don't know how to behave on the field and might damage our reputation". He also added that he had asked certain star players to "spread the word around".

Sports writer Harry Done was in complete agreement – "Sterner action by referees and linesmen is one solution, but clubs could help if they ignored big reputations and followed Creek's example by pointing a warning finger at the culprits," he said. Norman knew how he wanted football to be played – skilfully and fairly. As Mike Greenwood, who played in many of Norman's international teams, said, "He expected strict adherence to the laws of the game. Even retreating ten yards for a free kick had to be done quickly, without any shenanigans".

The ten years that Norman was at the helm of

English amateur football were difficult ones. Factors outside his control were changing world football, but he determinedly stuck to his Corinthian values. Steve Menary felt he was either naïve or content to ignore the problems, while Brian Wakefield, the reserve goalkeeper at the Rome Games, said, "He was so very honest, and thought everyone else was the same". Those of his former players I have had contact with are all agreed he was a 'very nice person' and a gentleman. Some even looked upon him, as one put it, as a 'kindly, pipe-smoking uncle'.

Norman was a coach of players, not a modern–day manager of teams. He did not go in for tactical team talks but looked to improve the play of individuals by quiet one to one talks and instruction. He was very good at man management and interested in the psychological aspects of the game and the players – all within a framework of fair play and sportsmanship. Unfortunately this framework was being eroded by money and the over-riding desire to win at almost any cost. That, Norman would not embrace.

CHAPTER TEN

A FULFILLING RETIREMENT

1963-1980

In 1963, Norman reached the normal retirement age of sixty five. His last match in charge of the England Amateur team was scheduled to be on 28th September 1963 at The Oval, Belfast, against the amateurs of Northern Ireland. The sporting press made much of this 'end of an era'. As Michael Styles wrote, "England's amateurs will be functioning for the last time tomorrow as 'Creek's Mob' – the impolite but affectionate label attached to the national side in amateur soccer circles since Norman Creek took charge early in 1955".

Michael Melaniphy stated what all English observers were agreed upon: "By winning, England can give a great send-off to team manager Norman Creek in his last international before he retires. It is the only fitting salute to Creek and his brilliant record as manager".

Victory for England might have seemed fitting for the

end of an era, but it was not to be - the Northern Ireland players spoilt the party by winning 2-1. However, there was to be a final victory for Norman. Because of a delay in his successor taking up his post, he was asked to stay on as manager of the Great Britain team for the first of the qualifying matches for the Olympics, which were to be held in Tokyo in 1964. This match was against Iceland in Reykjavik. It was almost 'Creek's Mob', as the squad of fifteen players consisted of fourteen Englishmen and one Scot (fullback Willie Neil of the Queens Park club). Recent games against Iceland had seen England victorious by two clear goals, but this time it was a most decisive 6-0. "It's amazing the difference one Scot can make!" quipped Norman afterwards.

The return match at Wimbledon's Plough Lane ground was easily won 4-0, and the 10-0 aggregate score set up Great Britain for a two-leg second qualifying round with Greece. That was the end of Norman's international management – Charles Hughes was now in place. As it turned out, it was also the end of Britain's hopes of reaching the finals in Tokyo, as they lost 5-3 on aggregate to Greece.

With the end of his FA work, Norman and Lilian moved house once more, this time to 'Cheverells', Godwyn Gardens, in Folkestone. They both loved the south coast, and their daughter Heather and her family lived at Ash, near Sandwich, only fifteen miles away. But Norman's remark to his players at a presentation in his honour that he "wouldn't be donning his tracksuit again" proved incorrect. Early in 1964, the Football Association of Thailand decided that to improve the quality of the game in their country they needed to improve the expertise of their coaches. They approached FIFA (the International Association Football Federation, football's world governing body, who recommended Norman to them). A week later the 'flying sportsman' was on his way to spread the word.

During an eighteen-day course at Chulalongkorn University, Bangkok, Norman lectured and gave practical demonstrations to over a hundred and twenty-five coaches from all over the country. The Thai FA secretary spoke of the success of the venture, "not just for us in Thailand", but also hailed it as "a step forward in the advancement of Asian football".

Returning from this coaching stint, Norman assumed he would have time now to help Lilian arrange their new home for their retirement years. But the world of football was still not ready to let him go. The Bermuda Football Association team were to make their first tour abroad (to Iceland), and they contacted the English FA for someone qualified to train and coach their squad. Denis Follows, the FA secretary, recommended Norman to them. At first he was reluctant to accept. As he explained to the BFA secretary, John Rosewarne, this was to be a six-week course, and he had only recently returned from almost three weeks in Thailand. "My wife will have almost forgotten what I look like!" he told him.

That objection was quickly overcome when the invitation to visit the island was extended to include Lilian. The *Bermudan Times* reported, "Tomorrow Bermuda soccer will enter a new era when Norman Creek steps from a London jet at the Civil Air Terminal". Norman wasted no time in getting to work with the players. On the first day, behind locked doors to keep the fans away, at the stadium in Hamilton, the squad played a full-scale practice match. Norman simply observed the first half but refereed the second, stopping play to bring out certain points. At the end of this first game, he gathered all the players together to give a recap of the points he had made. Afterwards he told the BFA officials how pleased he was with the physical condition of the players, as well as their enthusiasm.

In his coaching sessions he was at pains to praise and encourage each of the players and bolster their self-belief. But he stressed the importance of ball control and concentration – "There is only one grass pitch in Iceland. The rest are lava based and players must be able to control the ball quickly and must not mentally 'switch off' in a game". He was also concerned that their exuberance was causing them to play a hectic, kick-and-rush type of game. "You are doing everything at one pace – fast. I am looking now for one or two players who can hold the ball and at times slow down the play. Varying the speed gives you more options", he told them.

Besides individual ball work to improve skill and

maintain fitness, in the last two weeks there were several group sessions for the forwards and defenders, concentrating on play in the penalty area. "That's the place where it really matters", Norman explained to local journalist Gordon Robinson. "If they don't know how to build, or stop, an attack in midfield by now, they never will".

At the end of the final training session, Norman was presented with an engraved silver tray and a cedar inkstand and pen by the chairman of the Bermuda Football Association, who said, "There can be no doubt we selected the right man for the job. Our soccer owes him a debt of gratitude".

Three days later Norman and Lilian arrived back in Folkestone, and this time Norman really did put his tracksuit away.

The 1965-66 season proved to be a momentous one for English football – The World Cup was hosted by England. Norman followed the progress of the tournament avidly and then, when England reached the final, he was there at Wembley Stadium (Row 7 Seat 7) as an invited guest of the FA. Their win against West Germany greatly pleased him and he was gratified to note that several of the England squad had in earlier years played schoolboy and youth international matches when he had been in charge of those teams.

That was his final involvement with the FA in any semi-official or honorary role, but he couldn't walk away from sport completely, for sport ran in his veins. For the next decade he wrote match reports on south coast football teams (particularly Brighton and Hove Albion, which had always been his favourite team), and in the summer, cricket summaries of the home games of Hampshire, Somerset and Gloucestershire for the *Daily Telegraph*. He threw himself into these retirement years as energetically as he had in every other phase of his life. Time was not to be wasted, except that now the family were the main beneficiaries.

Lilian was in charge of arranging the house just as they wanted it, but the garden became Norman's particular preserve. He now had the time to be more than just a fairly interested potterer and became a very keen gardener. His grandchildren, Lucy and Jamie, who lived near enough to visit fairly often, recall that the garden was always undergoing improvements, and was kept immaculate. Ever the perfectionist, he did not tolerate weeds; so much so that a neighbour, for a joke, put a little weed in an envelope and posted it through his letterbox with a note saying he'd found it in his front garden!

He fell into a regular daily routine, the first part of which was doing the cryptic crossword in the *Daily Telegraph*. Then, weather permitting, it was gardening, a walk along the seafront or a drive out in their car. Norman wasn't a keen driver, but he ensured the car was well maintained at the local garage and polished until it gleamed. However, Lilian was very happy to do more than her share of the driving. As a young woman, she had been keen on machines. In the 1920s she had a

Vincent motorbike until, after she had come off it when taking a bend too quickly (on her way to see Norman play football) he had insisted she give it up. However, the car enabled them to visit their daughter, Heather, her husband Barry and their children, Lucy and Jamie, more easily.

Every so often they treated themselves to two or three days in hotels, mainly in southern England, with Cornwall (Penzance), South Wales (Tenby) and Goring-on-Thames being particular favourites. Longer holidays were spent abroad, with Northern Italy their favoured destination in Europe.

In 1959 their son Carey had moved to a teaching post in Vancouver Island, Canada, and, in 1963 he married Kixi, the school nurse, who had been born in Colombo, Ceylon. By 1970 they had four children, Hamish, Benjamin, Nicola and Kanina, so several times in the 70s Norman and Lilian made the long journey to spend time with them.

The qualities which had brought Norman such success in all his endeavours – meticulousness, quiet enthusiasm and encouragement of others - now found expression in his family life. He found time to help his son-in-law with the garden at their house at Ash. He levelled and prepared a stony piece of ground to make a lawn enlisting the help of Lucy and Jamie (five and three) by giving them a small bucket each and seeing who could pick up the most stones in half an hour. He relished the role of grandfather. "He always involved us in any way he could, showing that life could be both fun and serious at the same time", Lucy recalled.

Jamie and Lucy obviously had more contact with their grandfather than their Canadian cousins, and they have special memories of him. "He was very patient and helped me understand fractions, which I'd had trouble with at school", recalls Jamie. Later, when trigonometry was proving to be something of a mystery to him, "He brought it to life for me. Knowing that I adored sailing, he started asking me things like – 'What's the angle on the clew of this spinnaker?' It all became relevant to me then".

Jamie also remembers how, when he asked his grandfather about when he had played football or cricket as a young man, "he always turned the conversation round to how I was doing at rugby or sailing". In 1978, when Jamie had taken up the sport of windsurfing, he would phone Norman to check on the tides, wind and sea conditions at Folkestone – "The reports I received from him were always very detailed, precise, and his predictions accurate". All the grandchildren treasured the little poems he used to write for them on 'important' occasions. These were always in his own small, neat handwriting, never typed. The passage of over forty years has inevitably resulted in many of them being lost, but three of them have survived and are reproduced here, two for Lucy (one for her gaining entry to Simon Langton School; the other when she was voted Captain of Form) and one for Jamie (when he was hoping to be chosen for his school cricket team).

Norman was also a generous and selfless grandfather. The Christmas after Lucy was twelve, Norman gave her and her 'Granny' an envelope each containing tickets for the two of them to go to visit Carey in Canada that summer. Lucy realised that one of the tickets had originally been for him, but he would have none of it. Then when Lucy was 18, Norman and Lilian decided to give up driving and they gave Lucy their car, a pale blue Austin 1100. Norman had always been a cautious driver and he passed on to Lucy various tips, such as not exceeding 48 mph to extend the life of the vehicle!

Lucy also recalls, "As Jamie and I got older we realised just how much Grandpa adored Granny. He would secretly book a holiday and then announce it to her as a surprise – and she would be thrilled (even if she wasn't!) They were very much in love and always tried to sit next to each other wherever they were so that they could hold hands or at least touch each other".

Norman was still spritely in 1973 (in that year John Morgan, the *Daily Express* Sports writer of the year, when he interviewed him at 'Cheverells', commented on his being able to run up the twenty steps to his front door, taking them two at a time!) But by 1976 they had moved to the seafront at Clifton Gardens, a more easily managed apartment.

They had both been churchgoing people all their

lives, and Norman, in this last decade, having more time available, did a great deal of church work at Holy Trinity Church in Folkestone.

After a life which he filled almost to overflowing, it was in many ways a blessing that Norman's final illness should be short. He died at his Folkestone home on 16th July, 1980. The funeral service was held at Holy Trinity Church. His obituary in *The Times*, as well as listing his various career achievements and honours awarded, stated: 'He departed as he had lived, peacefully, for he was the kindly, gentle soul with a ready laugh who always sought the best in people and things'.

In the Holy Trinity with St George's church magazine of September 1980, the vicar, The Reverend S E Crawley, wrote:

For many years Norman stood in the lectern on Remembrance Day and read the passage that begins 'Come let us praise famous men'. Wearing the insignia of the MBE, the Military Cross and campaign ribbons, he had every right to call us to remember those who did not return from the wars. Many of us were surprised to learn from the obituaries in The Times and Daily Telegraph just how distinguished a career he had had as a sportsman, schoolmaster, pioneer broadcaster and journalist. This was one of the delightful things about Norman, we never heard it from his own lips, because right to the end he was so much more interested in other people's achievements than his own. We at Holy Trinity remember him for what was not mentioned in the Press: his long service as a Reader, Sidesman, and a Church Councillor.

I would like to add a personal tribute. Right from the start I felt a particular affinity for Norman Creek. This was partly because, although separated by a full generation, we had much in common. My father was also a schoolmaster, an international sportsman and a journalist. Many of his close friends were Norman's friends also. But it was deeper than that. I knew by his spiritual appreciation and encouragement that here was a kindred spirit, and his very presence was an inspiration.

A more recent letter from the Rev. Crawley states:

Norman was a modest and honourable man, a lay reader who led worship with simple integrity without posture or pretence. He was the essence of middle of the way Anglicanism at its best. I count his friendship as one of the most enduring and valued memories of my time as Vicar of Holy Trinity Folkestone. In all this he had a wonderful and true companion in his wife Lilian.

Three years ago, when I started researching the life of F N S Creek, I knew little about the man. I have been helped by many people, but it has not been easy to fully appreciate the true measure of this remarkable person. Over and over I found people who had known him in one field of endeavour who were unaware of his other achievements. He was an exceptional man and a very modest one. I hope this book will bring the wider recognition he deserves.

VERSES

Written by FNS to his grandchildren

~~~

Dear Jamie, since the end of term
I've had a note about a worm
This little worm ate all he could
That's why his Christian name is 'Wood'.

'Anonymous' tells how he dares
To eat up all his grandpa's chairs.
No wonder Grandpa has a frown
Without a seat for sitting down!

I'm sending you a photo that
Will show you how to hold a bat.
I'm sure no woodworm does repose
Upon the bat of Brian Close.

Just study this – see how he stands,
Look at his wrists, his arms, his hands.
So reach right forward – take the plunge –
With bat in hand, just try a lunge.

But watch the ball, that piece of leather
And always keep your hands together.
Then you'll be thrilled to highest heaven
When you play for your school eleven.

~~~

The weather at New Year is always so cold,
With gales and with frosts and with snowstorms untold,
But what does it matter if there is a storm –
When little Lucinda is Captain of Form?
She went to school early for her second term
With hopes and ambitions, determined and firm;
Her friends gathered round her like bees in a swarm,
And promptly elected her Captain of Form.

She set off last Wednesday by car and by bus,
Her hair and her dimple were quite glamorous;
And looking so sweet in her school uniform –
No wonder they voted her 'Captain of Form'.

I'm sure she will do the job thoroughly well,
And troubles and riots immediately quell.
So here's 'All good wishes and sentiments warm
To darling Lucinda – the Captain of Form'.

~~~

I was in the bedroom shaving – it's a job one can't postpone –
When at 9.15 precisely came a ring upon our phone:
And Lucinda told us proudly of the news we'd never banked on
How she'd heard that very morning that she'd passed for Simon Langton!

Like her we almost cried for joy to hear such splendid news,
Though the soap around my nostrils made it hard to air my views.
So in case I didn't manage to convey my great delight,
I'm sending you this little ode to put the matter right.

We hardly thought at Iver as we pushed you in your pram
That ten years later you'd do well to pass a stiff exam.
Perhaps this is the starting point for greater things in store,
Certificates at 'O' and 'A', Matric., degrees galore.

I'm sure you will remember that as Jamie follows you -
And Hamish, Ben and Nicola have places in the queue –
They'll all be looking up to you as if you were a sample,
That's why we hope you'll always be a wonderful example.
So good luck, darling, when you start at S.L. in September,
I'm sure that like your grandpa, you always will remember
The day when at eleven years old, a letter came to say
You'd passed your first important test – so HIP HIP HIP HOORAY!

THE CREEK FAMILY TREE

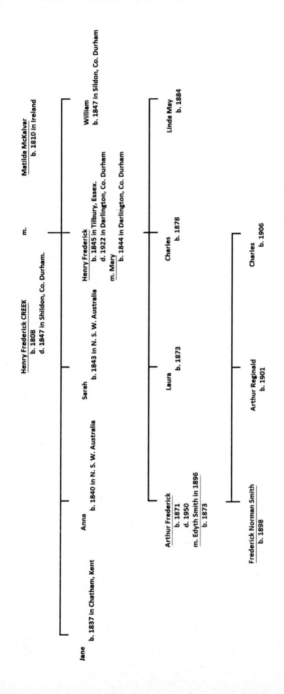

Henry Frederick CREEK
b. 1808
d. 1847 in Shildon, Co. Durham.

m.

Matilda McKalvar
b. 1810 in Ireland

Jane
b. 1837 in Chatham, Kent

Anna
b. 1840 in N. S. W. Australia

Sarah
b. 1843 in N. S. W. Australia

Henry Frederick
b. 1845 in Tilbury, Essex.
d. 1922 in Darlington, Co. Durham
m. Mary
b. 1844 in Darlington, Co. Durham

William
b. 1847 in Shildon, Co. Durham

Arthur Frederick
b. 1871
d. 1950
m. Edyth Smith in 1896
b. 1873

Laura
b. 1873

Charles
b. 1878

Linda May
b. 1884

Frederick Norman Smith
b. 1898

Arthur Reginald
b. 1901

Charles
b. 1906

THE DESCENDANTS OF FNS CREEK

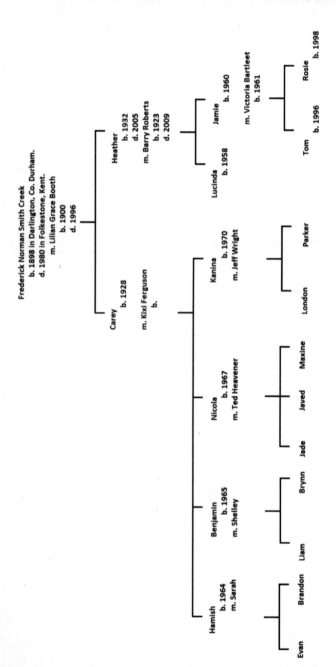

Frederick Norman Smith Creek
b. 1898 in Darlington, Co. Durham.
d. 1980 in Folkestone, Kent.
m. Lilian Grace Booth
b. 1900
d. 1996

Heather
b. 1932
d. 2005
m. Barry Roberts
b. 1923
d. 2009

Jamie
b. 1960
m. Victoria Bartleet
b. 1961

Rosie
b. 1998

Tom
b. 1996

Lucinda
b. 1958

Carey
b. 1928
m. Kixi Ferguson
b.

Kanina
b. 1970
m. Jeff Wright

London

Parker

Nicola
b. 1967
m. Ted Heavener

Jade

Javed

Maxine

Benjamin
b. 1965
m. Shelley

Liam

Brynn

Hamish
b. 1964
m. Sarah

Evan

Brandon